SONG OF THE AVATAR
Visual Riffs on the Bhagavad Gita

By Gary Whitney

Foreword by Elesa Commerse

Copyright © 2019 Gary Whitney

All rights reserved

Printed in the United States of America

First Printing, 2019

ISBN: 978-1-54396-927-6

For more info or groups please write to:
visualriffs@gmail.com

In Memory of
"Mystic Mary"
Mary Elizabeth Whitney, née Kaudy
Swami Namakirtanananda
1952-2015

Om Shanti Shanti Shantih

Contents

Dedication.....*i*
Contents.....*ii*
Foreword.....*iii*
Acknowledgments.....*vi*
Preface.....*vii*
Prelude.....1
Chapter 1 - Arjuna's Despair.....14
Chapter 2 - The Sage.....22
Chapter 3 - Spiritual Action.....40
Chapter 4 - Acting with Wisdom.....54
Chapter 5 - Renunciation.....67
Chapter 6 - Meditation.....77
Chapter 7 - Wisdom.....92
Chapter 8 - Eternal Reality.....112
Chapter 9 - Wisdom on the Path.....122
Chapter 10 - Divine Splendor.....140
Chapter 11 - Krishna's Cosmic Form.....164
Chapter 12 - The Path of Love.....177
Chapter 13 - Tilling the Field of Karma.....187
Chapter 14 - Spiritual Evolution.....202
Chapter 15 - The Higher Self.....210
Chapter 16 - Two Paths.....218
Chapter 17 - Faith.....224
Chapter 18 - Compassion in Action.....230
Coda.....250
Epilogue.....253

Foreword by Elesa Commerse

Yoga is skillfulness in action.

Swami Satchidananda taught, "Scriptures ought to be read again and again…If any of the lines catch your eye and your heart, read them often. Learn them by heart and apply them in your life. You don't even need a whole sentence, not even half a sentence. Just a quarter of one line is enough to lift you like a rocket, not just to the moon or Mars, but to the heavenly sun itself."

Strap in. Get ready to travel through the cosmos of your inner universe, with a good guide. Prepare to experience the world around you with new vision, sans virtual reality goggles. Remove your shoes as you feel the holiness and sacredness of everything and everyone. Breathe deeply as you reclaim your place in the eternal family of Oneness.

What lies within these pages is a delightful cracking of the code of wisdom unrivaled; a visual masterpiece of one of the greatest holy scriptures ever recorded for our benefit. Born in India, between 400 BCE and 200 CE, like the Vedas and the Upanishads, this Beloved Lord's Song, known as *The Bhagavad Gita*, was created to end our bondage.

It is said that Mahatma Gandhi recited the entire second chapter of the *Gita* as part of his daily prayers. The last eighteen (18) verses became the foundation of his morning and evening meditation practice. They anchored his mind in stillness and informed him at the deepest levels. From this place of discernment, he ordered his steps while teaching the world that non-violence is the way.

As a meditation teacher, students often come to me lamenting that they want to be free. I can relate. I want to be free, too. With compassion, I look into them and whisper, "Darling, how free do you want to be?"

"Why is it so difficult to make progress on the path?" they ask. I come a little closer and say with compassion, "Because the path has to go through you, Beloved."

Everyone is in the midst of their soul's journey. Knowing this, we should aspire and work hard to be as free as we can be, resting in the truth that Martin Luther King, Jr. uttered, "I can't be who I ought to be until you are who you ought to be." We inter-are, you and I, along with every other being in the world.

Our greatest endeavor as a spiritual warrior is the wearing away of all that is not the essential Self.

Most of us spend most of our lives enslaved, ensnared by false perceptions of reality and value; beset by ignorance and darkness that take the form of disturbing emotions, obscurations, pain and suffering. These become cycles, patterns of samsaric delusion, that steal our life, our peace of mind, our joy and our sanity.

It is considered a most auspicious moment – when the student meets the teacher. I was blessed to experience such a moment in 2001.

I met Gary Whitney as a result of seeking counsel from his extraordinary and erudite wife, Swami Namakirtanananda, aka Mary Whitney, who, at the time, was the Temple Astrologer for the Temple of Kriya Yoga, in Chicago.

I had heard Mary speak at several of the Temple's noon meditations and every time I did I said to myself with amazement, there is no one on earth like the supremely gifted Mary Whitney. And then I met Gary. I started to attend the noon meditations every time he spoke as well. And I thought the same thing: there is no one on earth quite like the revelatory Gary Whitney. I felt entirely blessed to study at the feet of Mary and Gary Whitney. Every time I was in their presence or fortunate enough to be the recipient of one of their smiles, I felt a certainty of basic goodness, a penetrating type of healing and a deep renewal of my soul. I now know this was an energy transfer of pure bliss, pure light, pure unconditional love that can only come from an enlightened teacher.

So when I decided to share the beauty, intricacy and timeless treasure of *The Bhagavad Gita* with my students, I sought out the one person I trusted the most to make the teachings come alive. In 2010, Gary Whitney took me and my students on the deepest journey into the heart of *The Bhagavad Gita*. Over the course of the year, during Gary's talks, it was as if the characters had all gathered in that sweet circle we called sangha, held at the Carl Jung Center, on Dempster Street, in Evanston.

Our time together transcended the clock and by the end of each session, we would all look at each other wide-eyed and stunned as we made our re-entry, wondering what just happened; where did we go?! I felt like I had time traveled back to the days when Krishna and Arjuna met on the battlefield. All the characters became animated and I FINALLY learned how to pronounce their names!

I found new relevance and insight into current events. Happenings around and within me revealed new meaning. Gary helped me experience *The Bhagavad Gita* as a portal through which to better understand the most complex metaphysical phenomena in the most practical of ways. Repeatedly, I pinched myself to ensure I wasn't dreaming!

I was captivated by this great storyteller who conveyed bits of the journey as if he had been there himself. Now, many years later and after reading the book you hold in your hands, I believe Gary did go to Kurukshtra; and he took very good notes - with his whole self! Over the last seven years, Gary has drawn out, frame by frame, the journey to moksha. What a priceless gift!

This is no ordinary book – it is a labor of love! I encourage you to read it slowly. Savor the details in each offering of each drawing. Like individual beads on the perfectly strung mala, know that the images your eyes behold transmit the power of the mandala. They travel directly into your heartmind. There, they inform you at the deepest levels and as such have the power to help transform you.

Gary Whitney, through the deftness gained through decades of intense personal practice, discipline, inquiry, renunciation and study, has birthed a spiritual guide like no other. It is *The Bhagavad Gita* made real and friendly. There's even a sweet and soulful talking dog! I can feel the saints and sages of old rejoicing as they herald Gary Whitney's breakthrough work of art, *Song of the Avatar*.

This is the field manual for the spiritual warrior. Within the walls of this animated classroom, you'll learn the truth about life and death; about what character is made of. Complex yogic terms like maya, boon, gunas, yamas, niyamas, neti, neti, neti, pranayama, mantra, prakriti, purusha, karma, ahimsa, reincarnation, sat chit ananda, samadhi, nirvana and more are demystified and explained in ways that will cause you to say, "I get it." Get ready for your electric bill to go up because aha, lightbulb moments abound on every page. Moreover, you'll find clear meditation instruction for both sitting and walking. And you'll find the answer to the question, "What is the biggest mistake humans tend to make in their lives?"

Gary Whitney has given us the gift of hope with this volume that has no expiration date because it is timeless. Gary delivers the message that though we may feel lost, we are not lost. He has demystified the greatest scripture of the Indian continent and made it accessible to us with so much love that the light carried within each frame cannot help but penetrate the depths of our being.

May you be happy and know the roots of happiness. May you be free of suffering and the roots of suffering. May you be safe from inner and outer harm. May you live and let go with ease.

May you take refuge in the wisdom contained in every one of the more than 1,500 glorious images beneficently hand drawn and lovingly brought to life through great wisdom and insight by Gary Whitney, for the benefit of humankind, for they are meant to liberate you.

Do your part. Seek out a translation of *The Bhagavad Gita* that causes you to return to it again and again. Carry Gary Whitney's *Song of the Avatar* with you. Share it with others. Drink from its potent nectar often. Stay inspired.

Gandhiji said, "The soil of our mind has to be cultivated for the seed of truth to take such hold." You have in your hands a great tool that can help cultivate the soil of your mind. Now use it. Dive deep. Practice as if your life depends on it, for it does. Engrave these images into your heartmind. May you find yourself in the *Song of the Avatar*. May it become your love song. May you be as free as you can be.

Om Shanti Shanti Shantih

Elesa Commerse
Monday, January 21, 2019
Chicago, Illinois

Acknowledgments

Special thanks to my late wife, Mary, for her early support of this work. She was a true mystic, an expert astrologer, and my best friend for 45 years.

I would also like to thank my Guru, Goswami Kriyananda, who dedicated his life to building The Temple of Kriya Yoga in Chicago as a center for the study of spiritual wisdom.

Thanks as well go to Jay Lynch, cartoonist extraordinaire. I had the great honor of working with Jay for 12 years (1978-1990) illustrating *Phoebe and the Pigeon People,* the weekly comic strip that he wrote for *The Chicago Reader.* Jay was my cartooning mentor and a master crosshatcher, unsurpassed in his ability to wield a 4x0 Rapidograph pen.

In 1993, Monica Kendall and Ed Newmann hired me to work at their small company, Calabash Animation in Chicago. I worked there for the next 23 years. It presented many challenges by forcing me to learn how to apply (not always successfully) the dimensions of space and time to what I already knew of cartooning. Many thanks to all the people I ever worked with at Calabash, each one a teacher in addition to being a friend.

Thanks to Elesa Commerse for asking me to teach a 10-month course on *The Bhagavad Gita* for her Deep Study program in 2010. *Song of the Avatar* is based on the notes that I used for teaching that course. I also appreciate that she has taken the time to write the Foreword, a key ingredient of this work as a whole.

My gratitude also goes out to Apurva Ashok (formerly of Pressbooks), Mary and Mark Bushman, Cara Eakes and Emily Gooding at Biblioboard, Perry Fotopoulos, Andy Kamm, Frank Murray and Laona Fleischer at the Brookfield Public Library, Karen Schober-Maneely at BookBaby, and my dear friend Kathy.

Lastly, I would like to thank my grandfather, Ershel Ray Whitney, for encouraging me to draw. At a family reunion when I was five years old, he gave me a pencil and a piece of paper and asked me to draw a picture of his brother, Lee, who was sitting across the room. I worked hard on that drawing, and when I was finished my grandfather showed it to Lee and their brothers, Cliff and Orion. To my great surprise, these four usually dour and serious old men all started laughing. This experience taught me that drawings can make people happy, and was thus the beginning of my life's journey as a cartoonist.

Preface

Song of the Avatar is not a *translation* of *The Bhagavad Gita*. It is not intended to be a substitute or replacement for the *Gita*.

This book is more of a companion piece to *The Bhagavad Gita* - a new twist on the long tradition of *Gita* commentaries.

The concepts that are illustrated here have been primarily inspired by the teachings and commentaries of Goswami Kriyananda, Paramahansa Yogananda, and Eknath Easwaran.

Hopefully this book will move some readers to seek out *The Bhagavad Gita* itself, in one of its many translations.

-GW

Recommended reading:

Easwaran, Eknath: *The Bhagavad Gita* (Tomales, CA: Nilgiri Press); *The Bhagavad Gita for Daily Living* [Three Volumes] (Tomales, CA: Nilgiri Press).

Kriyananda, Goswami: *The Bhagavad Gita* (Chicago, IL: Temple of Kriya Yoga).

Prabhavananda, Swami: *The Song of God/Bhagavad Gita* (New York, NY: Mentor Books).

Yogananda, Paramahansa: *God Talks With Arjuna/The Bhagavad Gita* [Two Volumes] (Los Angeles, CA: Self-Realization Fellowship).

THE EVENTS LEADING UP TO THIS WAR ARE RECOUNTED IN THE *MAHABHARATA*...

...THE LONGEST EPIC POEM IN THE LITERATURE OF THE WORLD.

IT IS EIGHT TIMES AS LONG AS THE *ILIAD* AND THE *ODYSSEY* COMBINED...

...AND THREE TIMES AS LONG AS THE *BIBLE*.

THE *MAHABHARATA* TELLS THE STORY OF THE KURU FAMILY—DESCENDANTS OF THE GREAT KING BHARATA.

PANDU REIGNED AS KING FOR A TIME...

...BUT LEFT HIS THRONE IN ORDER TO LIVE IN THE FORESTS AS A MYSTIC.

PANDU'S BROTHER, DHRITARASHTRA, THEN BECAME KING...

...EVEN THOUGH HE WAS BLIND.

DHRITARASHTRA HAD 100 SONS WHO GREW UP WITH THEIR COUSINS, THE FIVE SONS OF PANDU — A.K.A. THE **PANDAVAS**.

YUDHISTHERA, THE ELDEST SON OF PANDU, **SHOULD** HAVE BECOME THE KING UPON PANDU'S EARLY DEATH...

...BUT SINCE HE WAS ONLY A BOY, HIS UNCLE CONTINUED TO RUN THE KINGDOM.

WHEN DHRITARASHTRA'S OLDEST SON, DURYODHANA, GREW UP, **HE** WANTED TO BE KING...

...AND PERSUADED HIS FATHER TO HELP HIM GAIN THE THRONE.

DURYODHANA TRIED TO KILL THE PANDAVAS BY ENTRAPPING THEM WITHIN A BURNING HOUSE

SNIFF

ARF! ARF!

WHA?

KOFF KOFF

# THE WAR THAT IS ABOUT TO BEGIN, HOWEVER, IS NOT KRISHNA'S BATTLE.

HE HAS VOWED **NOT** TO FIGHT...

...ALTHOUGH HE **DOES** WANT ARJUNA AND HIS BROTHERS TO WIN.

IN THIS WAR, KRISHNA'S ROLE IS TO SERVE ONLY AS ARJUNA'S CHARIOTEER AND ADVISOR.

THE **BHAGAVAD GITA** IS A CONVERSATION BETWEEN A WARRIOR AND HIS CHARIOTEER.

BUT ON A **DEEPER** LEVEL, IT'S THE DIALOGUE BETWEEN THE HUMAN SOUL (REPRESENTED BY ARJUNA)...

...AND THE ETERNAL REALITY (REPRESENTED BY KRISHNA).

THIS DIALOGUE TAKES PLACE IN THE DEPTHS OF MEDITATION, WHERE THE SOUL IS ASKING GOD QUESTIONS...

...AND INTUITION REVEALS THE ANSWERS.

THE **GITA** IS A HANDBOOK OF YOGA.

IT IS A PRACTICAL GUIDE FOR THE JOURNEY TOWARD ENLIGHTENMENT.

YOGA IS ABOUT THE UNION OF THE **FINITE** SELF, THE EVERYDAY MIND, WITH THE **HIGHER** SELF.*

*ETERNAL REALITY, INFINITE BEING, DIVINE SPIRIT, THE ATMAN, GOD.

THE SPIRITUAL PATH IS NOT THE PROPERTY OF ANY ONE RELIGION ALONE.

IT CAN BE FOUND IN **ALL** RELIGIONS, THOUGH IT MIGHT BE SOMEWHAT **HIDDEN**.

THE SPIRITUAL PATH IS NEITHER EASTERN NOR WESTERN.

ALL TRUE RELIGIONS WERE ORIGINALLY BUILT UPON THIS SAME FOUNDATION.

BRITISH AUTHOR, ALDOUS HUXLEY, CALLED THIS SPIRITUAL FOUNDATION **THE PERENNIAL PHILOSOPHY**.

UNDERLYING THIS WORLD OF CHANGE IS AN INFINITE, UNCHANGING REALITY.

...AND THAT THERE IS ONLY **ONE** PRODUCER FOR ALL THE DIFFERENT MOVIES IN THE MULTIPLEX.

PRODUCED BY **THE SPIRIT IN THE SKY**

THE GOAL OF YOGA IS FOR THE DIRECTORS TO REMEMBER **WHO** THE PRODUCER **IS**...

...AND TO "TAKE A MEETING" WITH THE PRODUCER VIA MEDITATION.

THE **BHAGAVAD GITA** IS ABOUT **REVERSING** THE PROCESS OF SPIRIT'S DESCENT INTO MATTER.

IT TEACHES HOW TO REASCEND FROM OUR LIMITED CONSCIOUSNESS AS MORTAL BEINGS...

...TO THE IMMORTAL CONSCIOUSNESS OF OUR **HIGHER SELF**...

...BECOMING **ONE** WITH THE **ETERNAL REALITY!**

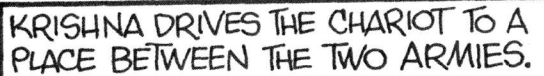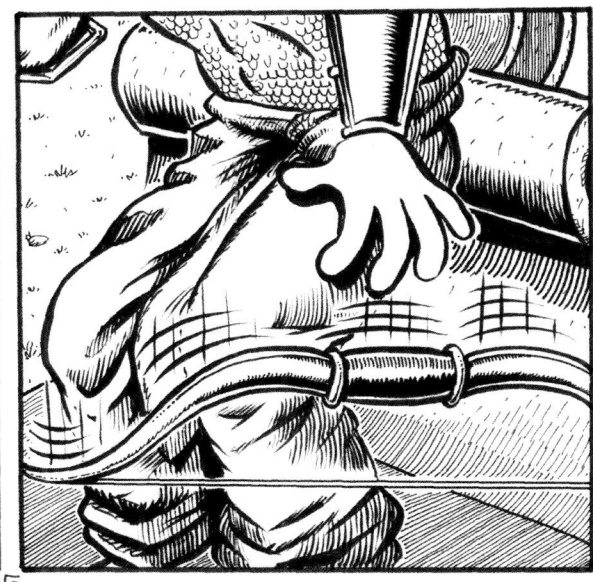

Facing the army of its desires, the individual soul first becomes aware of the spiritual plane of **DHARMAKSHETRA**, the field of **DUTY**.

On **THIS** field, all the desires of the past live again, armed against the soul... ...and the soul **KNOWS** that its duty is to **SLAY** those desires.

Kurukshetra is the field of action... ...the human body.

Every day, the battle between self-control and sense indulgence takes place on this field.

This is the conflict between the contentment and stillness of meditation...

...and the physical urge of the mind/body complex to get up and **GO**!

Our ultimate duty on the field of dharma is to **ATTAIN** and **SUSTAIN** enlightenment. In doing so, we free ourselves from the bonds of karma.

When Arjuna sees that the army of material desire must be slain, it brings him great sadness...

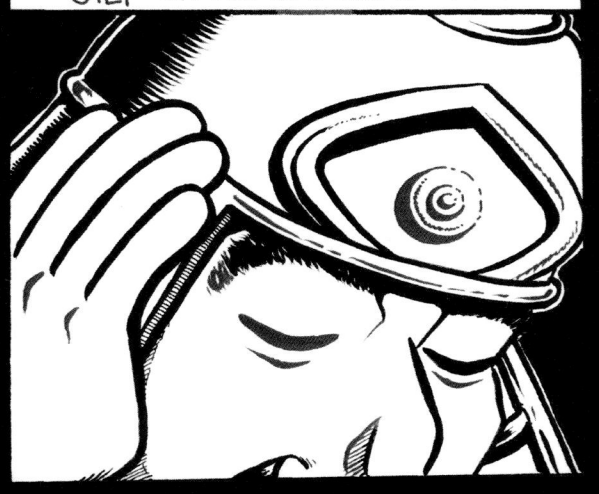

ARJUNA'S DESPAIR IS THE FIRST STEP ON HIS SPIRITUAL PATH.

THIS IS THE DARKNESS BEFORE THE DAWN...

...AND *IN* THIS DARKNESS, HE BECOMES AWARE OF A LIGHT *WITHIN*.

IT APPEARS AS A TINY STAR, TWINKLING IN THE DISTANCE.

BY THIS GLIMMER OF LIGHT, ARJUNA BEGINS TO SEE THAT THE WORLD OF THE EVERYDAY MIND MIGHT BE NOTHING MORE THAN ILLUSION...

...AND THAT THIS DISTANT STAR HOLDS THE PROMISE OF TRUE JOY!

IN THE ANCIENT FOREST TEACHINGS OF INDIA'S *UPANISHADS*, THERE IS A DESCRIPTION OF TWO BIRDS SITTING ON A TREE BRANCH.

ONE BIRD EATS THE FRUIT OF THE TREE, AS THE OTHER BIRD SILENTLY OBSERVES.

CHOMP! CHOMP!

THE TREE REPRESENTS THE BODY, AND THE EATING BIRD IS THE EVERYDAY MIND.

THE OBSERVING BIRD IS THE HIGHER SELF, THE **ATMAN**.

THE HIGHER SELF SEES **THROUGH** THE EYES...

...BUT CANNOT BE SEEN **BY** THE EYES.

ARJUNA AND KRISHNA ARE THE TWO BIRDS SITTING IN THE TREE.

WHEN ARJUNA QUESTIONED HIS STARTING POINT ON THE PATH, KRISHNA REMAINED SILENT.

THE VOICE OF THE DIVINE TEACHER, THE HIGHER SELF, HAS NOT YET BEEN HEARD.

BUT KRISHNA, THE SILENT BIRD, IS ABOUT TO BEGIN HIS SONG.

WHAT HE SINGS IS ONE OF THE MOST IMPORTANT SONGS THAT THE WORLD HAS EVER HEARD.

IT'S THE SONG OF THE AVATAR... ...THE ARIA OF THE COSMOS...

THE BHAGAVAD GITA

CHAPTER 2 - the SAGE

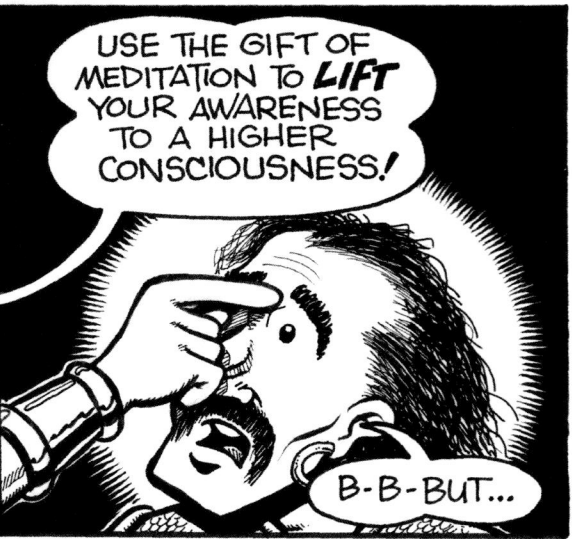

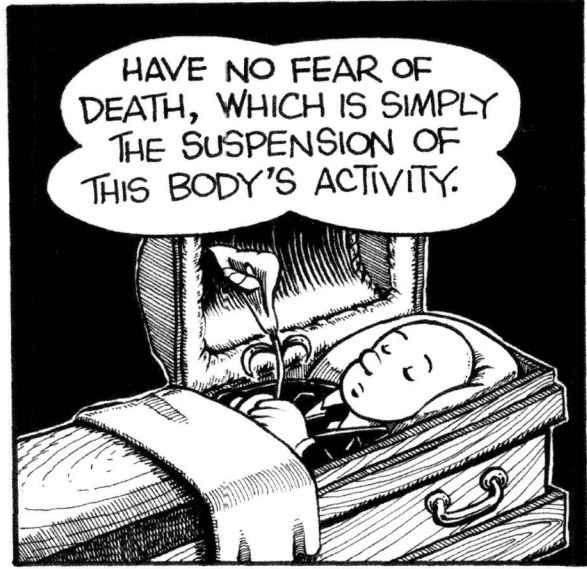

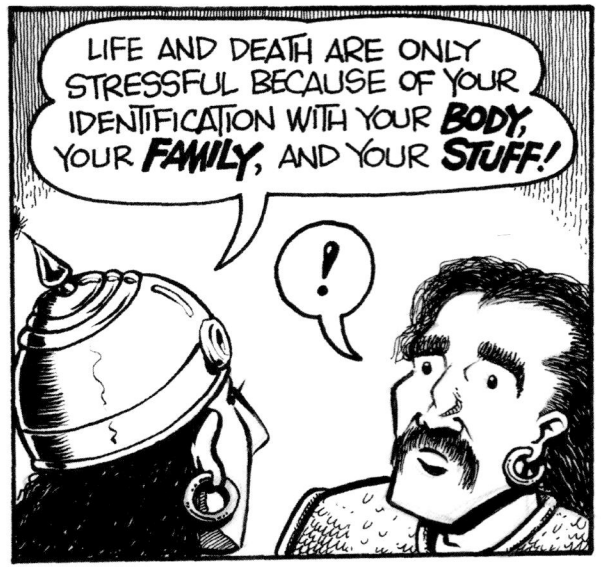

A GURU, OR SPIRITUAL TEACHER, WILL LIST THE BENEFITS OF WALKING THE SPIRITUAL PATH...	...AND THE STUDENTS WILL ADVANCE UPON THE PATH THROUGH THEIR PRACTICE.
THE *TEACHINGS* ARE CALLED *SANKHYA*...	...AND THE *PRACTICE* IS CALLED *YOGA*.

THROUGH YOGA, ONE LEARNS TO RISE ABOVE THE EGO-MIND, UNITING WITH THE **HIGHER SELF**... ...THE **ATMAN**.

THE YOGI THEREBY LOSES THE EGO'S DELUSION OF BEING **SEPARATE** FROM ALL OTHER FORMS OF LIFE.

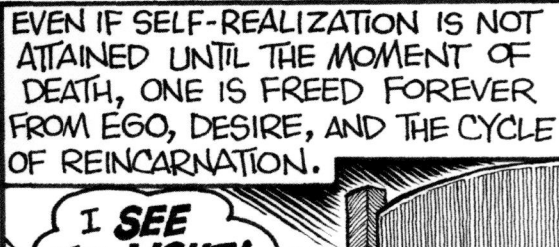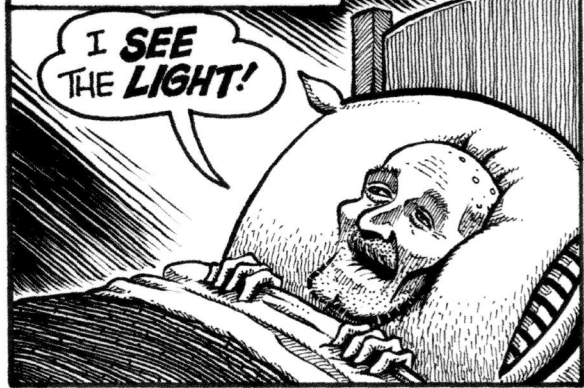

CHAPTER 3 — SPIRITUAL ACTION

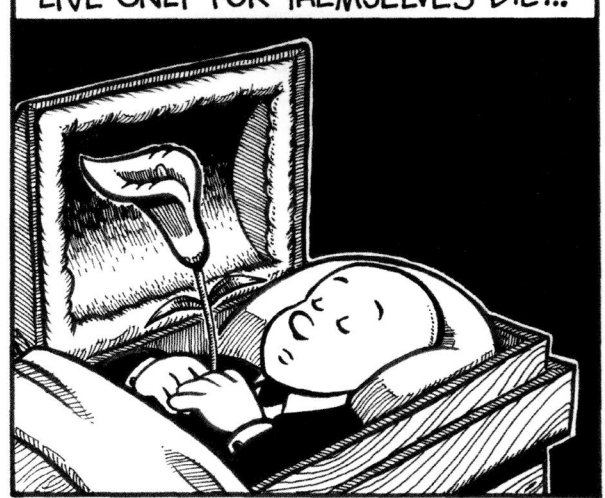

PEOPLE'S WORK CAN BE PART OF THEIR SELF-DISCIPLINE AS THEY WALK THE PATH.

ONE SHOULD TRY TO FIND A CAREER THAT DOES NOT EXPLOIT ANY LIFE FORM, IN ANY WAY.

DO NOT COMPARE YOURSELF WITH OTHERS.

RATHER, FOCUS ON DOING **YOUR** JOB IN THE MOST HARMONIOUS WAY POSSIBLE.

KRISHNA, CAN YOU TELL ME WHAT IT IS THAT MAKES ME LOSE SIGHT OF THE PATH, OVER AND OVER AGAIN?

WHY DO I PURSUE PLEASURE AND PROFIT WHEN I **KNOW** I SHOULD BE TRYING TO GROW SPIRITUALLY?

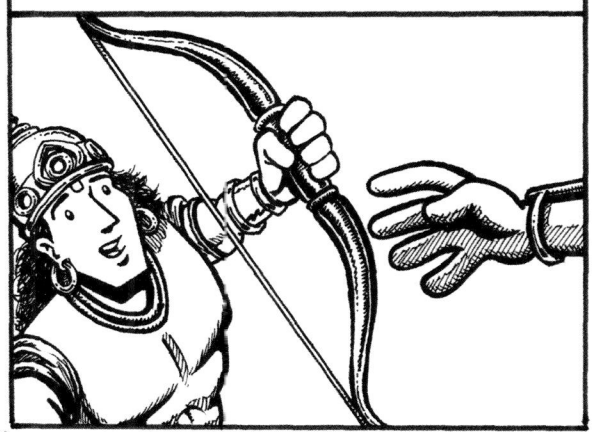

CHAPTER 4 — ACTING with WISDOM

Once upon a time, I taught yoga to a student named Vivasvat.

Vivasvat later passed these teachings on to a younger student.

Thus, yoga was handed down through generations. And today I teach YOU, Arjuna... ...because you are my friend.

But Vivasvat lived in ancient times, Krishna.

You and I are about the same age. How could you have been teaching THOUSANDS of years ago?

We have BOTH been born into this world many times, Arjuna.

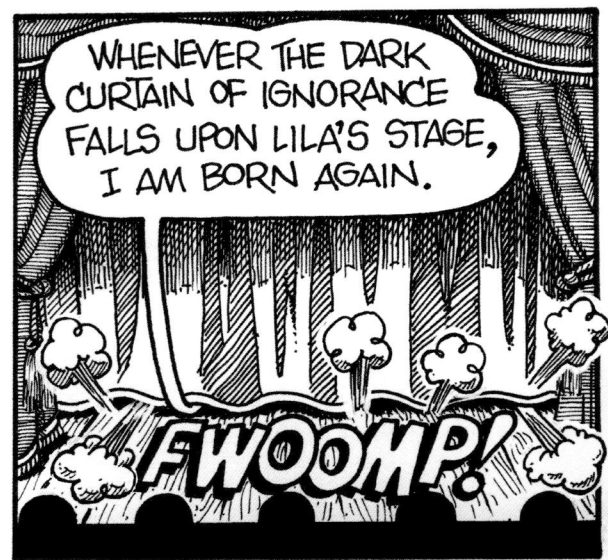

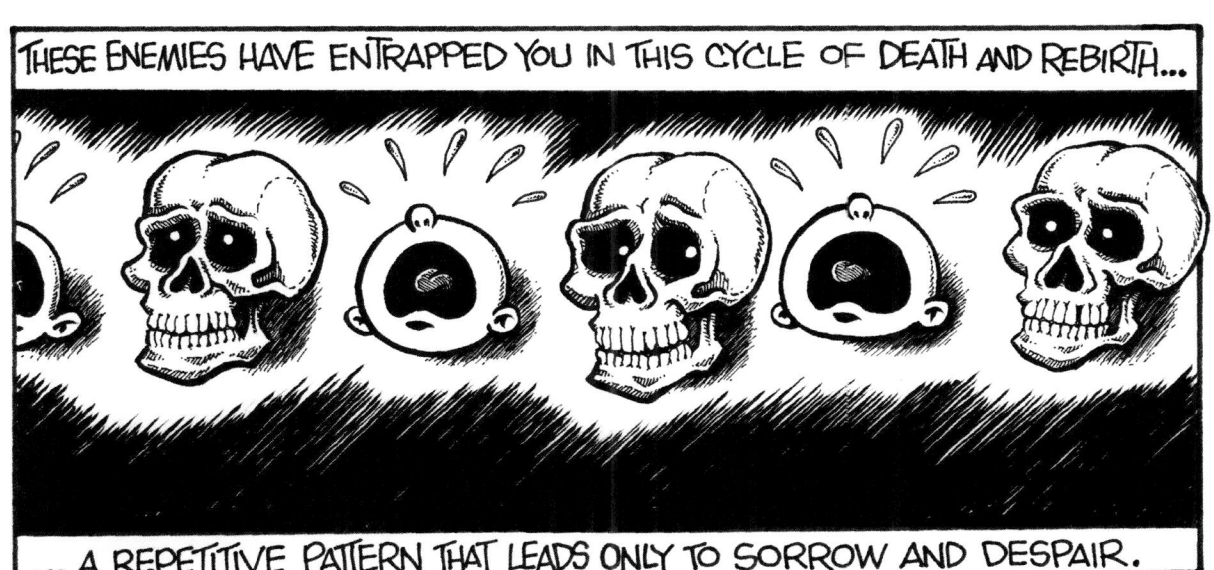

"Keep your body strong and healthy for selflessly serving others... and you will harmonize with the spirit that unifies all of life."

"When the ego dominates one's life, the mystical experience is not an option... and that unfulfilled life is one of frustration and insecurity."

"Fulfillment comes when one begins to serve others. Happiness will truly come when one learns to make OTHERS happy."

"There are different ways of GIVING. Some choose to give MONEY..."

"...some give MATERIAL goods..."

"...some will give their TIME and ENERGY..."

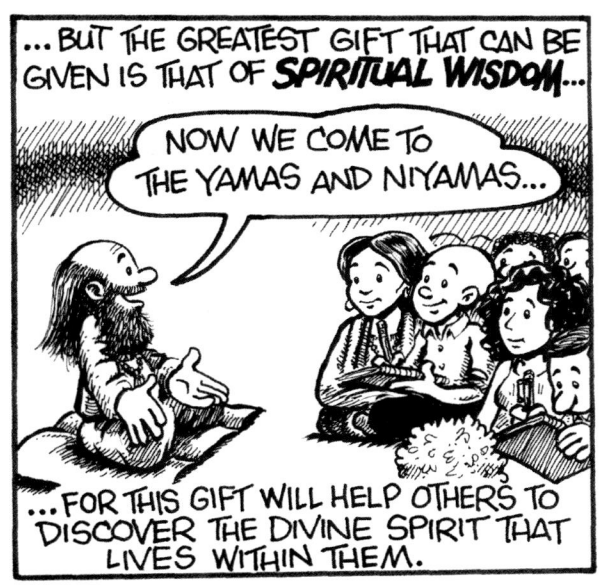

CHAPTER 5 - RENUNCIATION

FROM THE MUD AT THE BOTTOM OF A POND, NEW LIFE ARISES.

WHEN THE LOTUS REACHES THE SURFACE OF THE POND, ITS BLOSSOM REACHES TOWARD THE SUN.

THE GREEN LEAF OF THE LOTUS PLANT IS **RESILIENT** AND **WATERPROOF**.

WHEN PEOPLE CHOOSE LIVES OF SELFLESS SERVICE, THEY BECOME LIKE THE LOTUS LEAF — RESILIENT AND **TROUBLE** PROOF.

RRRIBBIT!

SELF AWARENESS BRINGS PEACE OF MIND THAT LIBERATES US FROM ANXIETY

NETI NETI NETI

TO FIND JOY IN LIFE, LEARN TO **HIDE** YOUR EGO IN A PLACE WHERE NEITHER YOU NOR ANYONE ELSE CAN **SEE** IT.

SPLASH

PEOPLE WILL MAKE MISTAKES, ARJUNA — AND **SOME** PEOPLE WILL ALWAYS MANAGE TO DO THE WRONG THING.

IS IT **BAD** TO MAKE MISTAKES?

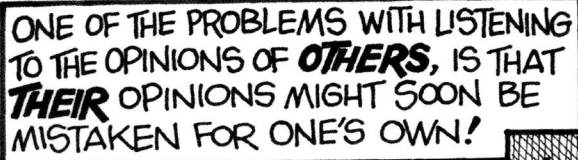

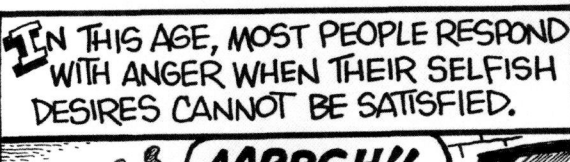

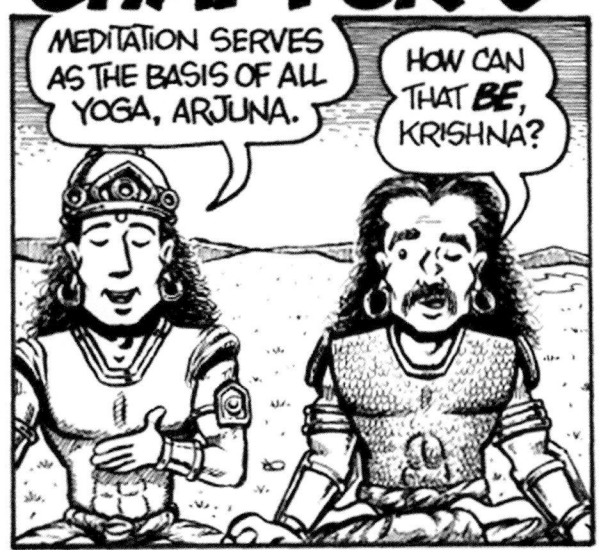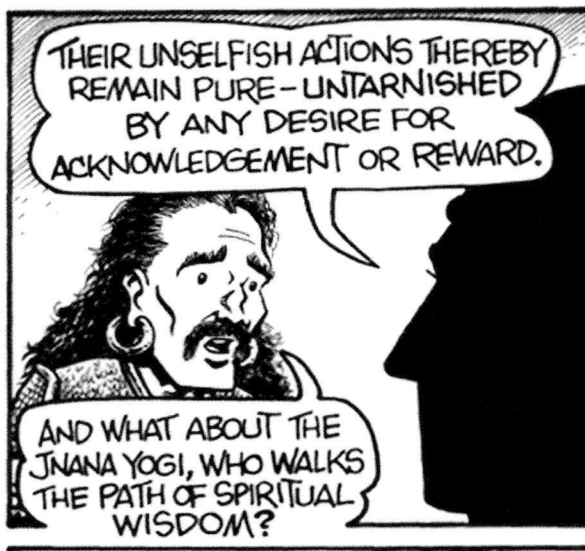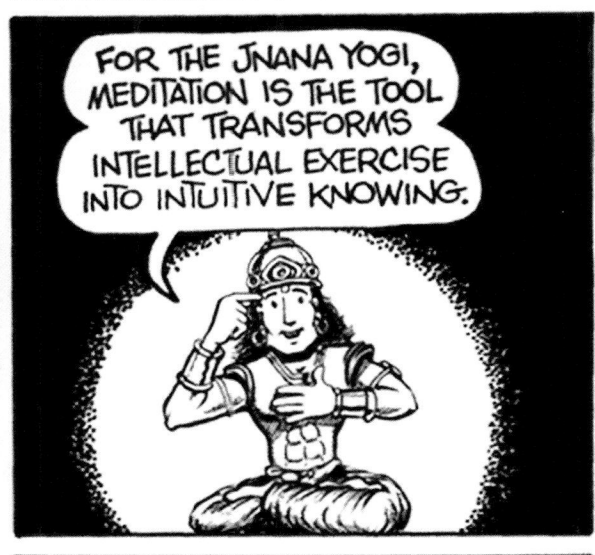

THE INDIAN MYSTIC, MEHER BABA (1894-1969), CALLED CHEERFULNESS A DIVINE VIRTUE.

PERHAPS HIS MOST PROFOUND TEACHING IS THE DECEPTIVELY SIMPLE SLOGAN: DON'T *WORRY* - BE *HAPPY!*

PARAMAHANSA YOGANANDA (1893-1952) RECOMMENDED A FORM OF KARMA YOGA THAT *EMBRACES* CHEERFULNESS.

BECOME A *SMILE MILLIONAIRE!*

ANYONE CAN BE A SMILE MILLIONAIRE JUST BY GIVING AWAY FREE SMILES TO EVERYONE THEY MEET.

SMILING DOESN'T *COST* YOU ANYTHING.

YOUR PERSONAL SMILE BANK ACCOUNT CONTAINS *MILLIONS* OF SMILES...

...AND THIS ACCOUNT *GROWS* EVERY TIME YOU GIVE A SMILE AWAY!

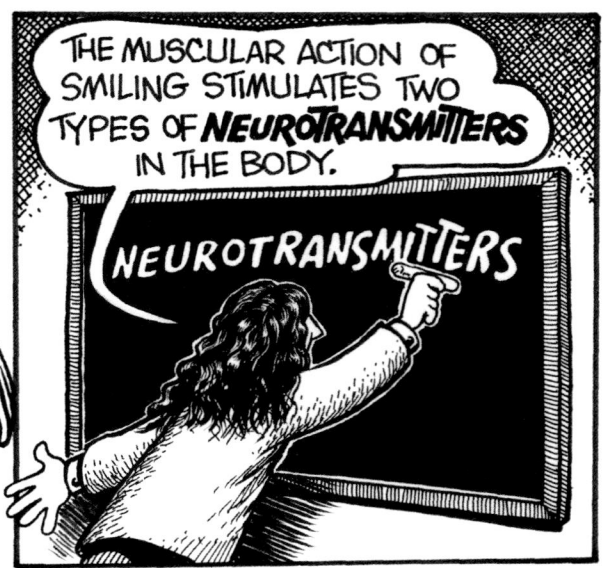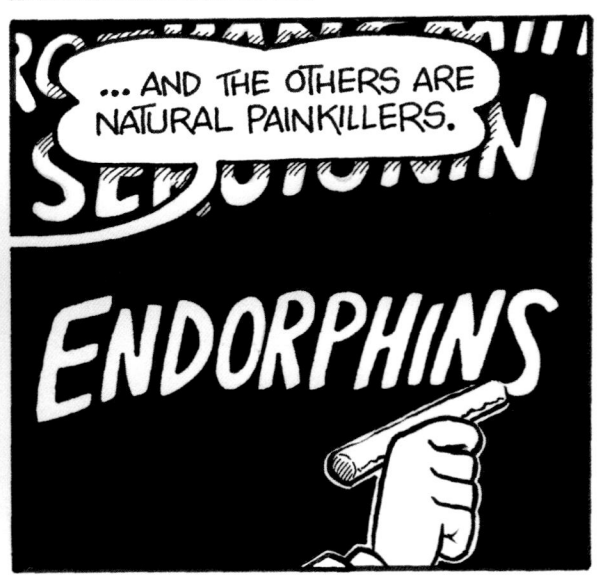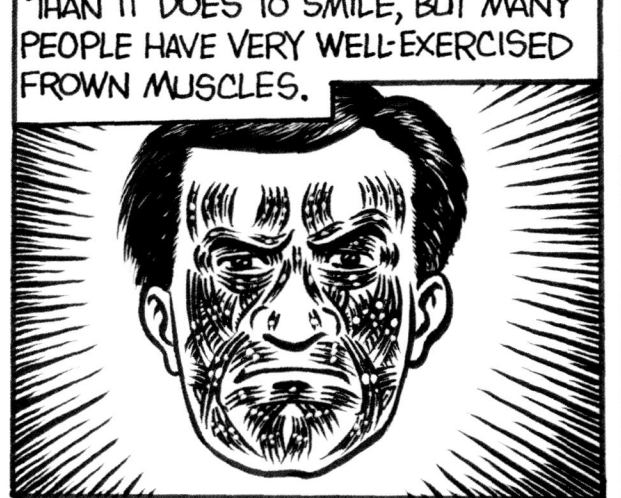

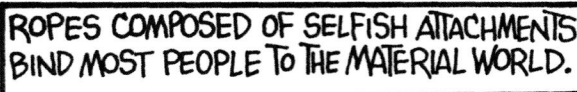

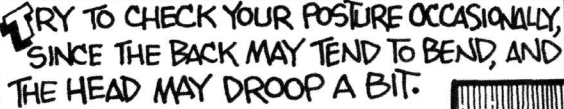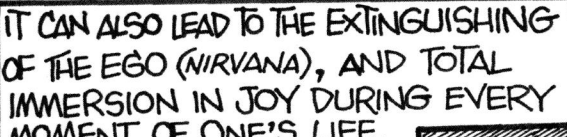

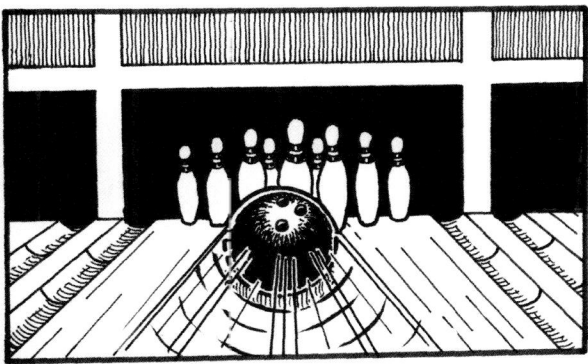
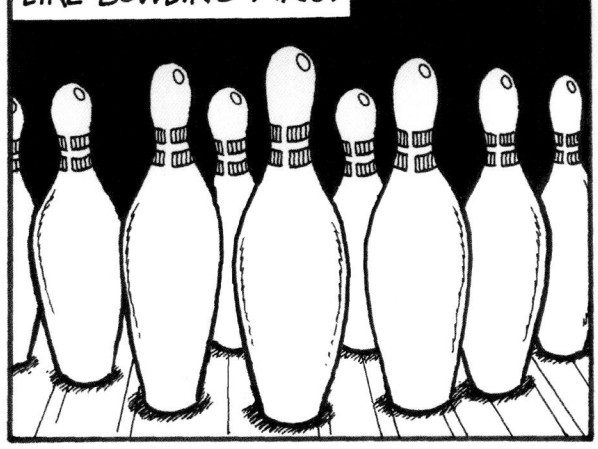

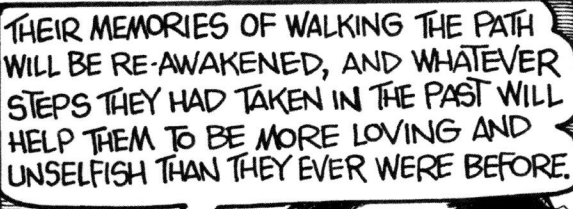

CHAPTER 7 - WISDOM

WALKING THE SPIRITUAL PATH IS NOT SOMETHING THAT INTERESTS MOST PEOPLE.

AND VERY FEW OF THE PEOPLE WHO WALK THE PATH ATTAIN THE GOAL OF ENLIGHTENMENT IN A SINGLE LIFETIME.

MY CHELA — IT WILL TAKE YOU AS MANY LIFETIMES TO BECOME ENLIGHTENED AS THERE ARE LEAVES ON THIS TREE ABOVE US.

ATTEMPTING TO STOP THE MOTION OF THE MIND IN MEDITATION GOES **AGAINST** NATURE, AND MOST PEOPLE DO NOT HAVE THE DISCIPLINE OR DEDICATION NEEDED TO EFFECTIVELY PURSUE THE PRACTICE.

BUT EVENTUALLY **EVERYONE** WILL REACH THAT HIGHEST GOAL OF SPIRITUAL WISDOM.

AND THIS IS WHY **PATIENCE** IS CALLED FOR ON THE PATH.

...AS MANY LIFETIMES AS THERE ARE LEAVES ON THIS TREE.

PATIENCE WITH ONESELF AS WELL AS WITH OTHERS.

OKAY, ARJUNA — TIME FOR A **POP QUIZ!**

GROAN

IT'S THE SCENT OF THE EARTH, THE LIFE FORCE IN ALL LIVING THINGS, AND IT'S THE **EFFORT** OF THOSE WHO WALK THE SPIRITUAL PATH.

PURUSHA IS THE SEED OF CREATIVITY THAT GROWS IN EVERY CREATURE.

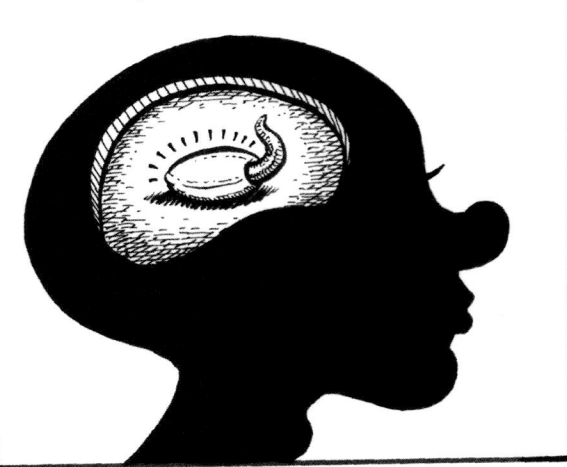

FROM THIS SEED, THE FLOWERS OF INTELLIGENCE, NOBILITY, AND STRENGTH BLOSSOM FORTH.

MEDITATION REMOVES THE WEEDS OF SELFISH DESIRE FROM THIS INNER GARDEN.

LORD VISHNU, THE PERSONIFICATION OF PURUSHA, SLEEPS ON A GIANT SERPENT IN THE SEA OF ETERNITY.

VISHNU DREAMS, AND THIS DREAM IS CALLED **MAYA**, MANIFESTING AS THE WORLD WE LIVE IN.

THE FABRIC OF MAYA IS WOVEN WITH THREE **QUALITIES** CALLED THE **GUNAS**.

SATTVA, RAJAS, AND TAMAS.

SOMETIMES TRANSLATED AS GOODNESS, ENERGY, AND INERTIA.

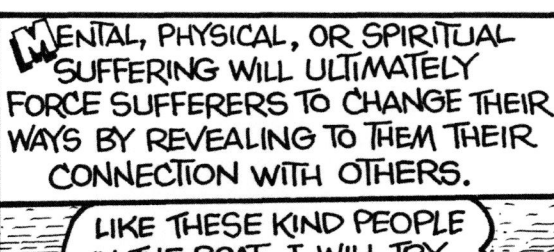

Those who walk the spiritual path, however, have chosen to give up their **OWN** ego expression in order to help and serve those who are still enmeshed within the grand illusion.

The spiritual seeker who has attained samadhi will see divine spirit existing in everyone and everything.

"And what **HAPPENS** to that awareness when they **DIE**?"

"People whose lives are entangled in the webs of karma and maya experience a disruption of consciousness at the time of death."

"The slate of their memory is wiped clean."

"But for self-realized sages there is **NO** disruption of consciousness when they die."

"They therefore **RETAIN** their awareness of the spirit that infuses all things."

"Does this mean that sages have **CHEATED** death?"

"It's more that the sage has gone **BEYOND** bodily death to the realms of conscious immortality."

There once was a young couple who prayed and prayed for a son who would be a devotee of Lord Shiva.

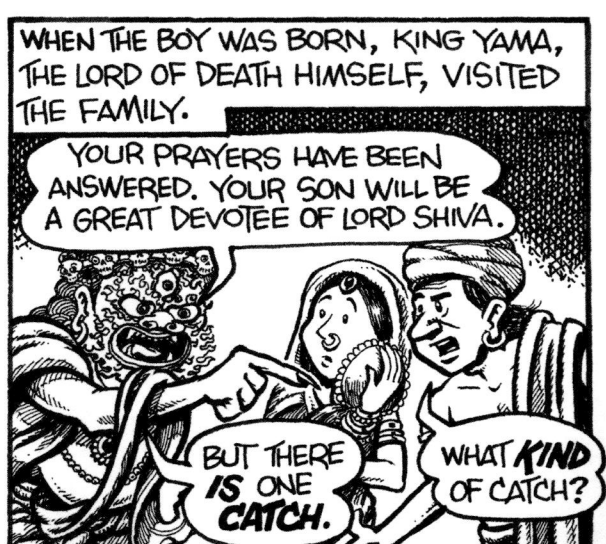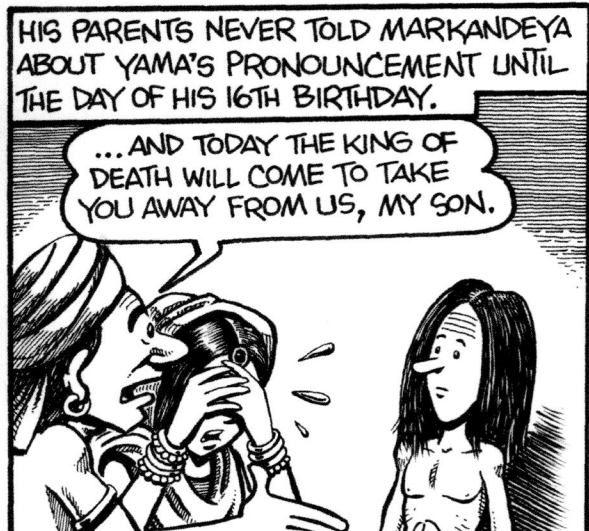

CHAPTER 8 — ETERNAL REALITY

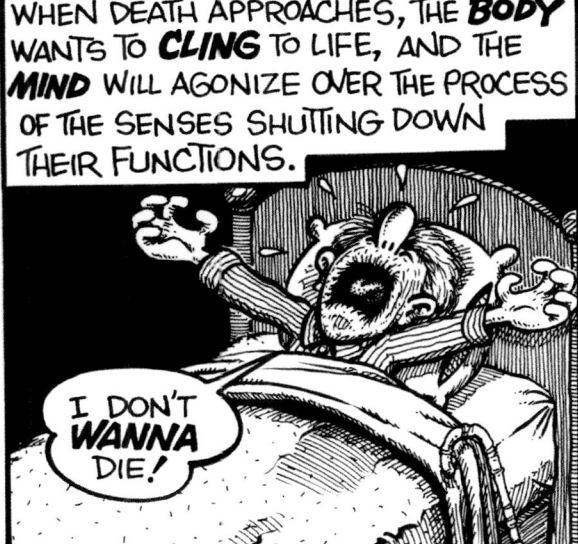

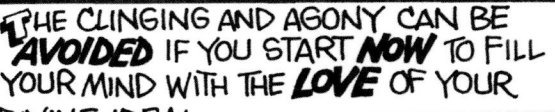

CHAPTER 9 - WISDOM on the PATH

This world of name and form, **PRAKRITI**, is moved through time by countless cycles of action and **RE**action.

And the **GOAL** of all these cycles, for humans, is the realization of the underlying **UNITY** that **CONNECTS** all names and forms.

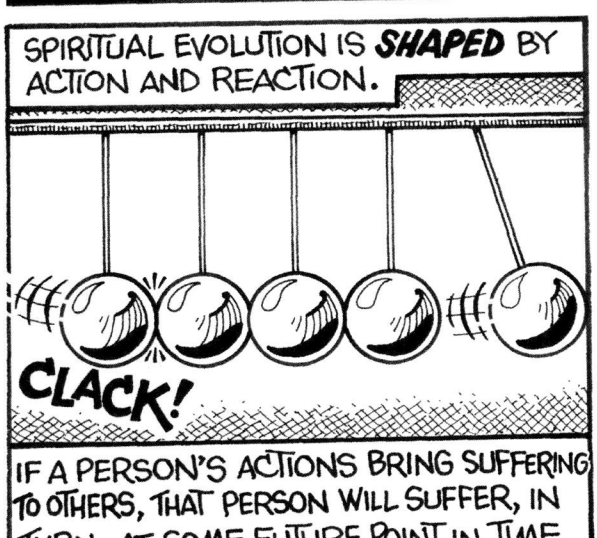
Spiritual evolution is **SHAPED** by action and reaction.

CLACK!

If a person's actions bring suffering to others, that person will suffer, in turn, at some future point in time.

This is the law of **KARMA**.

CLACK!

Or as some say, "What **GOES** around **COMES** around."

A Karmic Intermezzo

There are three types of karma.

The **FIRST** is what John Lennon called **INSTANT** karma.

Let's say that Curly **ACTS**...

HEY MOE!

NOW MOE IS NOT THE TYPE TO FORGIVE AND FORGET A THING LIKE THIS...

"WHY, YOU..."

...AND HE INSTANTLY **REACTS**, THEREBY **RESOLVING** THIS PARTICULAR PIECE OF KARMA.

FWOOSH

"MMMM— CHOCOLATE!"

"THE SECOND TYPE OF KARMA IS THE **REACTION** TO ONE'S **PAST** ACTIONS."

AND MOST LIKELY IT WILL BE *MOE* WHO THROWS THAT PIE.

MMMPH!

I'M A VICTIM OF SOY-CUMSTANCE!

NOT *REALLY*, CURLY. YOU'RE A VICTIM OF *KARMIC PAYBACK!*

THE KARMA DOESN'T *HAVE* TO COME BACK FROM THE PERSON WHO *ORIGINALLY* GOT OUR PIE IN THEIR FACE.

THE *REACTION* MIGHT NOT EVEN OCCUR IN THE SAME LIFETIME AS THE PRECIPITATING ACT.

AND THAT BRINGS US TO THE *THIRD* TYPE OF KARMA.

THIS IS THE KARMA THAT WE'RE CREATING RIGHT *NOW*, IN THE PRESENT MOMENT.

TIC TIC TIC

IF WE LOOK BACK AT THAT MOMENT WHEN CURLY HIT LARRY WITH A PIE, WE SEE THAT LARRY'S FIRST REACTION IS TO GET EVEN.

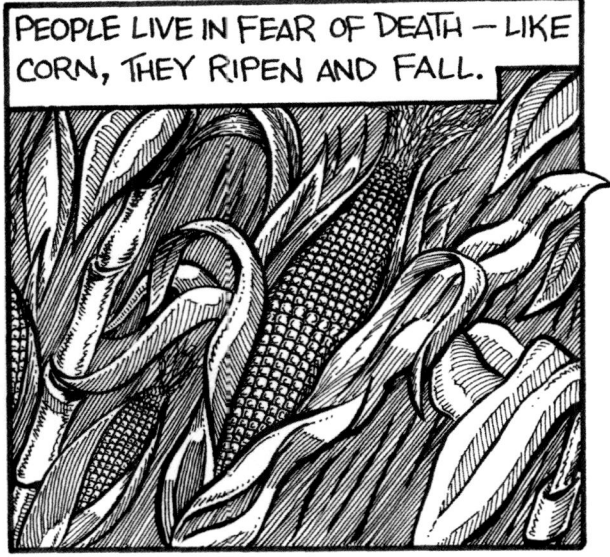

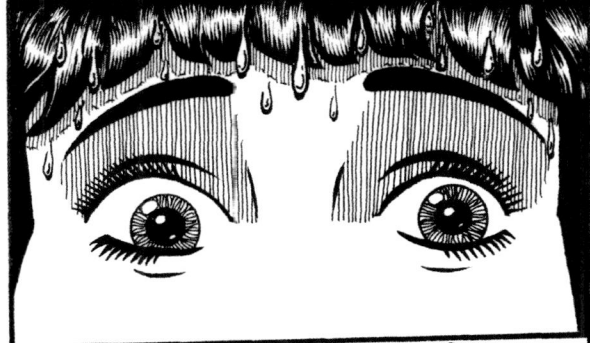

CHAPTER 10 – DIVINE SPLENDOR

DO YOU EVER GO TO THE **MOVIES**?

ONE, PLEASE.

IF YOU'VE EVER SEEN A **WESTERN** OR A **DETECTIVE** MOVIE, YOU'VE PROBABLY SEEN SOMEONE WHO HUNTS FOR CLUES.

THESE CLUES ARE USED TO TRACK DOWN THE **BAD** GUY.

OR A MISSING **GOOD** GUY— OR **GAL**.

WHATEVER.

THE TRACKER OR DETECTIVE IN THE MOVIE IS ABLE TO DISCOVER CLUES THAT OTHERS HAVE **MISSED**.

A-HA!

CLUE

IN THE STORY OF **THE RAMAYANA**, INDIA'S EPIC MASTERPIECE, RAMA'S WIFE, SITA, IS KIDNAPPED BY THE KING OF THE DEMONS.

HELP!

SHE DROPS PIECES OF HER JEWELRY FROM THE DEMON KING'S FLYING CHARIOT, HOPING THAT RAMA WILL BE ABLE TO DISCOVER THESE CLUES AND COME TO HER RESCUE.

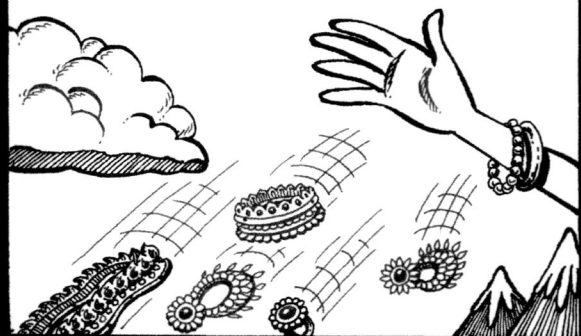

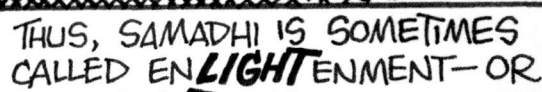

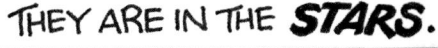

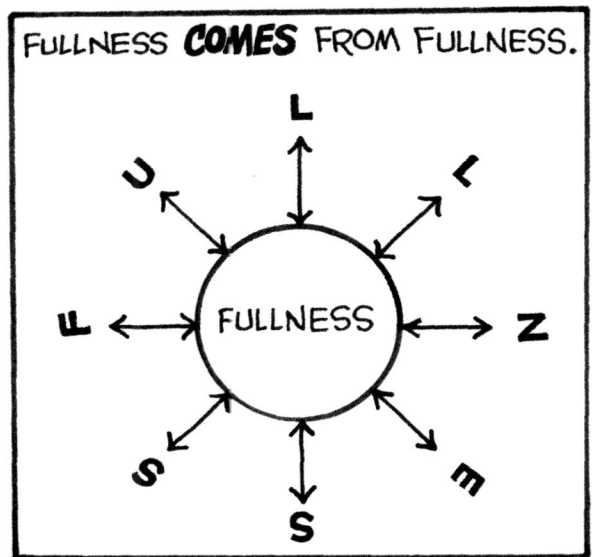

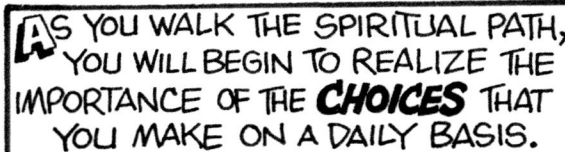

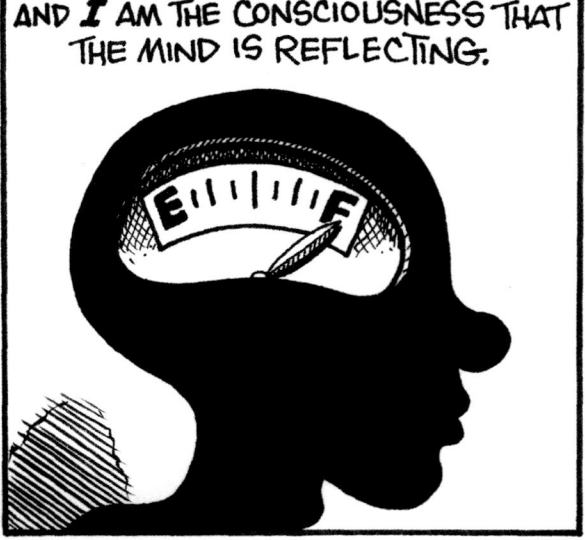

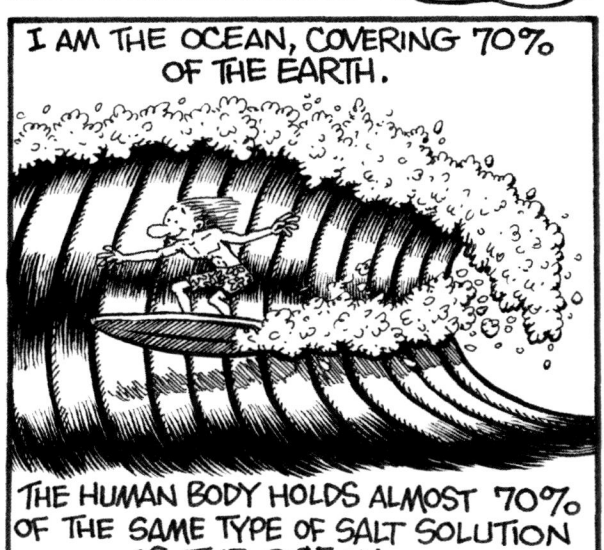

ONE CAN GET **LOST** IN LISTS THAT CATEGORIZE DIVINE SPLENDOR, AS WELL AS ALL THE NAMES AND FORMS COMPRISING THE MATERIAL UNIVERSE.

ULTIMATELY, SUCH LISTS DON'T MATTER.

ALL YOU **REALLY** NEED TO BE AWARE OF IS THAT ETERNAL REALITY **IS** PRESENT WITHIN EVERY LIVING THING.

REMEMBER THIS, AND ACT ACCORDINGLY.

LET DIVINE SPIRIT FILL YOUR MIND, ARJUNA, AND AVOID THE DISTRACTIONS OF MAYA.

WHEN YOU BECOME **UNITED** WITH DIVINE SPIRIT, IN WHATEVER FORM YOU **ATTUNE** TO, YOU WILL HAVE ATTAINED THE ULTIMATE **YOGA**.

LIFE WILL BE **GOOD**, BOTH MENTALLY AND PHYSICALLY. YOUR INCREASED INTUITION AND CREATIVITY WILL HELP YOU TO RESOLVE YOUR KARMIC PROBLEMS.

ON THE SIMPLEST LEVEL, JUST REMEMBER **ME**, AND KNOW THAT I **SUSTAIN** THE ENTIRE UNIVERSE, WHICH IS BUT A TINY **FRAGMENT** OF ALL THAT I AM.

AS A REMINDER, I'D JUST LIKE TO RE-EMPHASIZE THE IMPORTANCE OF USING THE SPIRITUAL MAGNIFYING GLASS OF MEDITATION FOR INVESTIGATING THE WORLD.

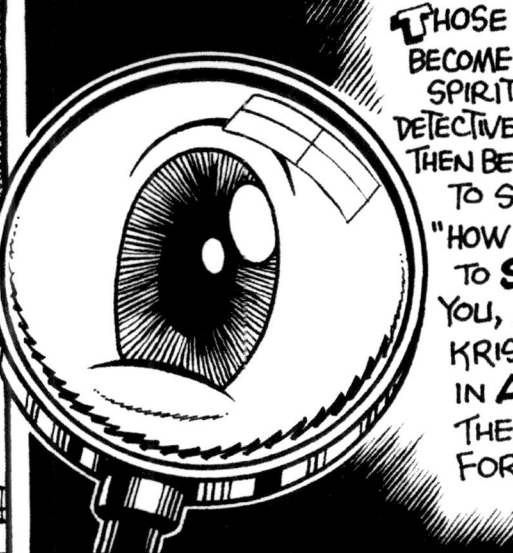
THOSE WHO BECOME GOOD SPIRITUAL DETECTIVES WILL THEN BE ABLE TO SAY, "HOW NICE TO **SEE** YOU, LORD KRISHNA, IN **ALL** THESE FORMS."

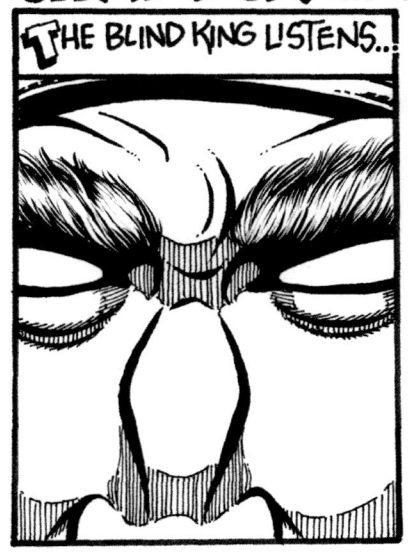

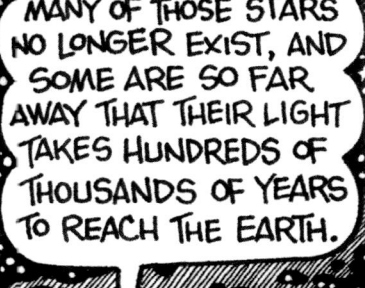

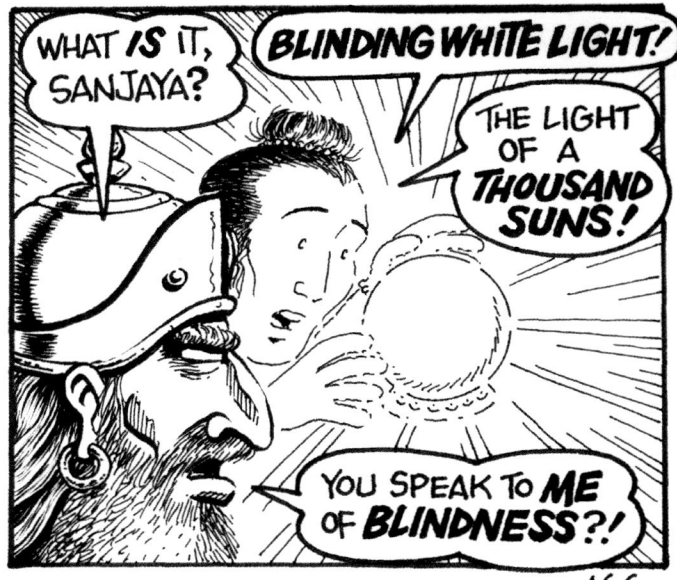

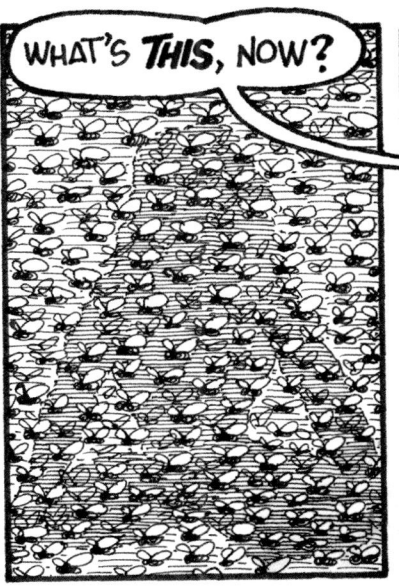

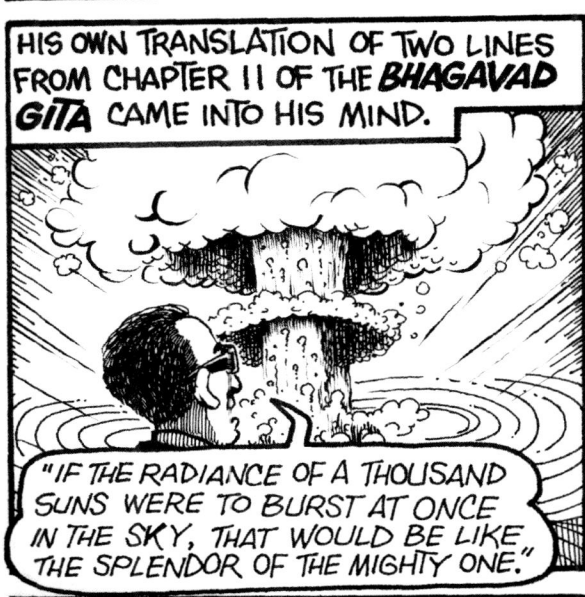

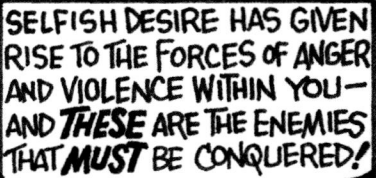

CHAPTER 12 - the PATH of LOVE

"KRISHNA..."

"AS YOU KNOW, I HAVE JUST EXPERIENCED YOGA — UNION WITH DIVINE SPIRIT THROUGH YOUR COSMIC FORM."

"PLEASE TELL ME THE BEST WAY TO ATTAIN YOGA AGAIN — IS IT THROUGH LOVE OR WISDOM?"

"LOVE FOR THE DIVINE IDEAL IS THE BEST WAY FOR MOST PEOPLE TO UNITE WITH ETERNAL REALITY, ARJUNA."

"AND ACCORDING TO THE SAGES, WE BECOME WHAT WE LOVE."

ONCE THERE WAS A MAN NAMED HARI WHO WAS TRYING TO LEARN HOW TO MEDITATE...

...BUT HE COULD NOT FOCUS HIS MIND.

HE ASKED HIS GURU FOR ADVICE...

"MEDITATION TROUBLE, EH?"

"YES, SWAMIJI. MY MIND WILL NOT STOP WANDERING."

177

HOW TO CATCH A MONKEY

1. CUT A SMALL HOLE INTO A DRIED-OUT COCONUT SHELL.

2. TIE THE COCONUT TO A FIRM OBJECT.

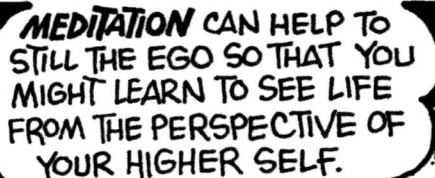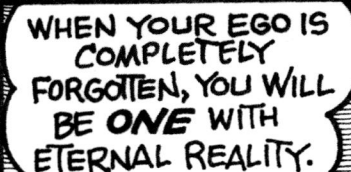

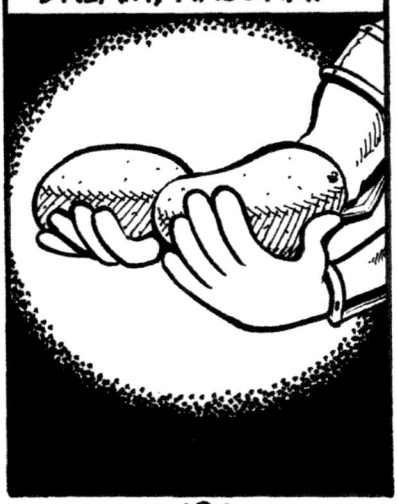

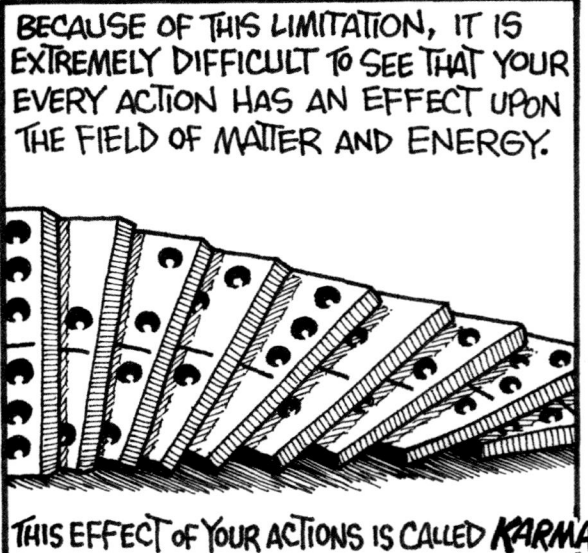

Every era presents a climate that is conducive to the ripening of karmic seeds that are shared by many of those who are living at that time.

You, as an individual soul, have incarnated many times in order to learn to change your responses to the events that life presents to you.

But you are ALSO part of a group of souls who tend to incarnate together to learn similar lessons on a larger scale.

While everyone shares the seeds of desire, anger, and fear, they also share seeds of wisdom, strength, and unselfish love.

Those who sow these latter seeds become beacons of light that others might follow.

Outside of time and space, Arjuna, there exists a cosmic seed-state of pure consciousness.

As the material universe evolves from this seed-state, so does the MIND.

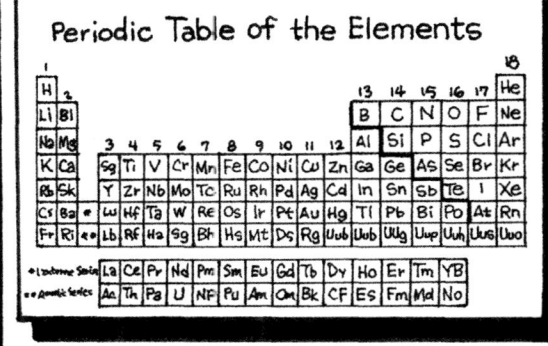
One part of the mind concerns itself with analyzing the universe...

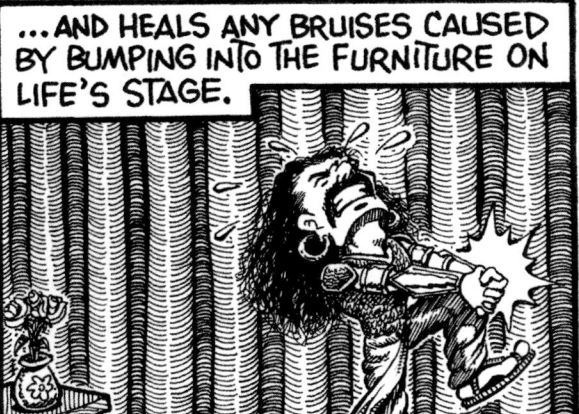

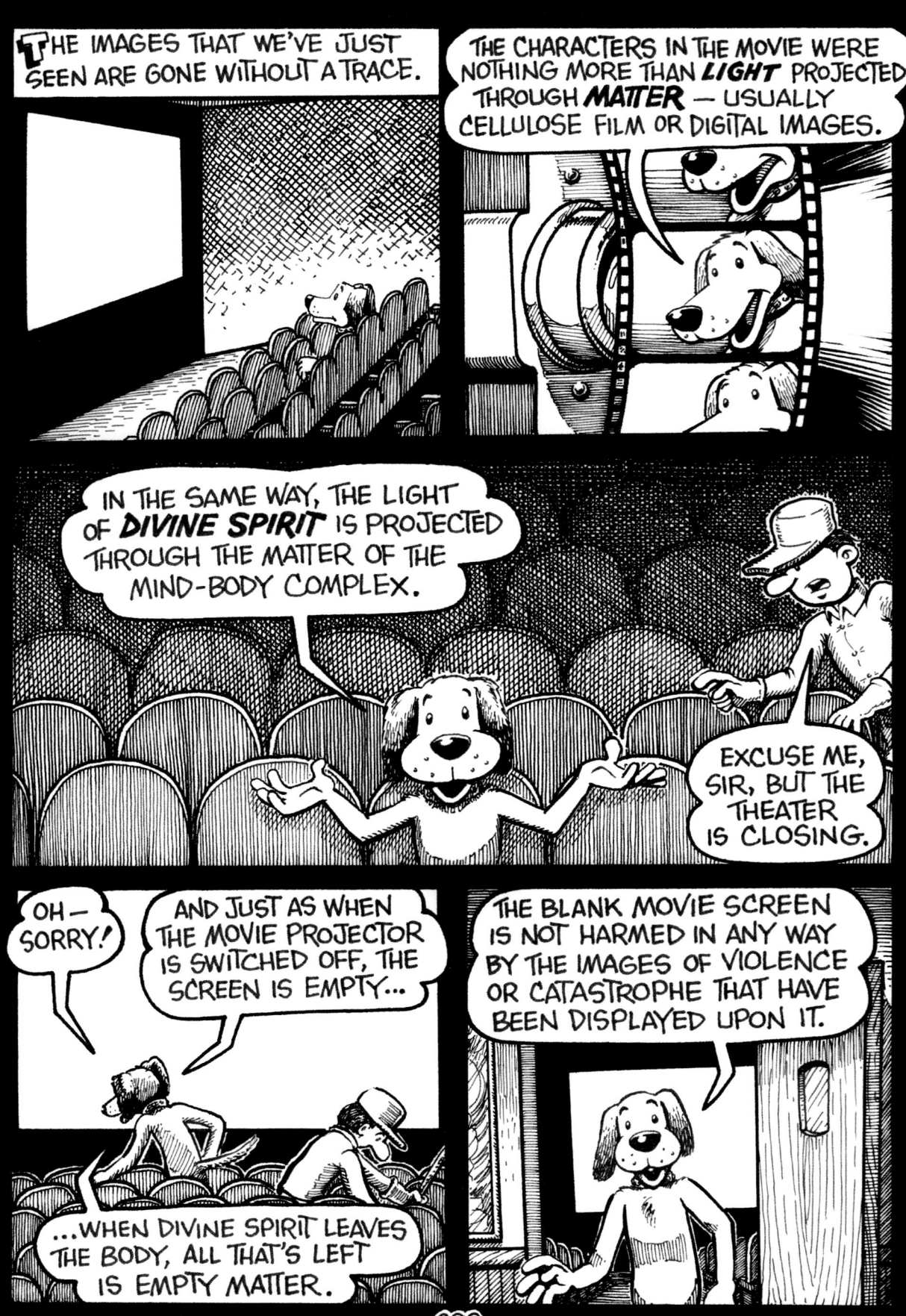

CHAPTER 14 – SPIRITUAL EVOLUTION

KRISHNA, I HAVE A PROBLEM.
WHAT IS IT, ARJUNA?

I—I'M AFRAID OF **DEATH**.
OH—IS **THAT** ALL?

THIS FEAR COMES FROM THE ERRONEOUS BELIEF THAT YOU ARE NOTHING MORE THAN YOUR MIND-BODY COMPLEX.
?

BUT AS I'VE BEEN TRYING TO EXPLAIN TO YOU ALL DAY, THE **REAL** YOU IS IMMORTAL SPIRIT.
THIS SPIRIT **CANNOT** DIE.

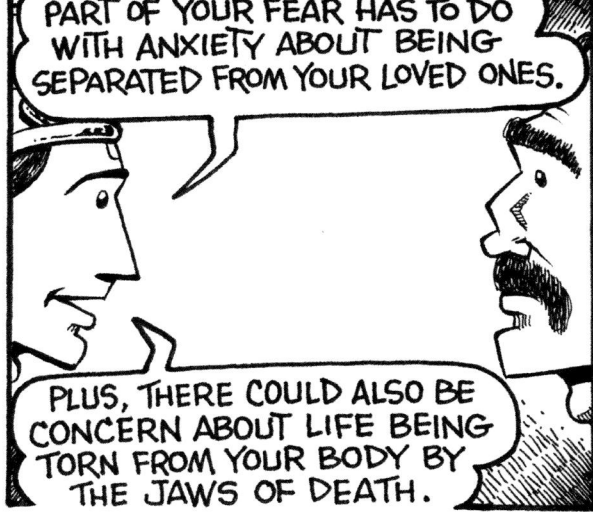
PART OF YOUR FEAR HAS TO DO WITH ANXIETY ABOUT BEING SEPARATED FROM YOUR LOVED ONES.
PLUS, THERE COULD ALSO BE CONCERN ABOUT LIFE BEING TORN FROM YOUR BODY BY THE JAWS OF DEATH.

MANY PEOPLE WHO FEEL THIS WAY WILL **CLING** TO LIFE NO MATTER HOW **SICK** THEY MIGHT BE.

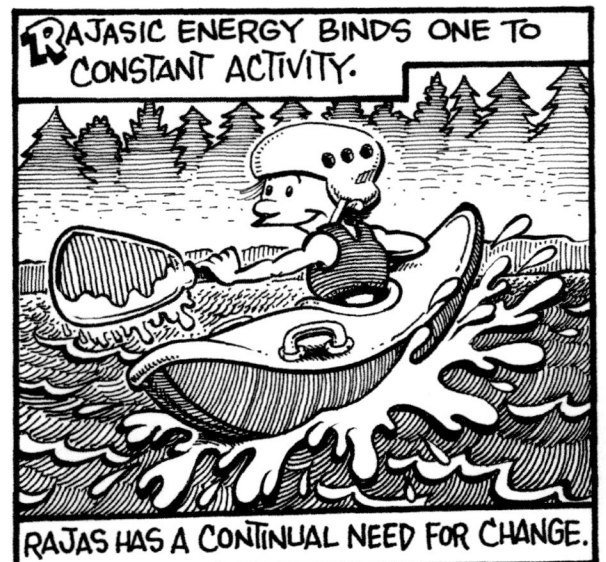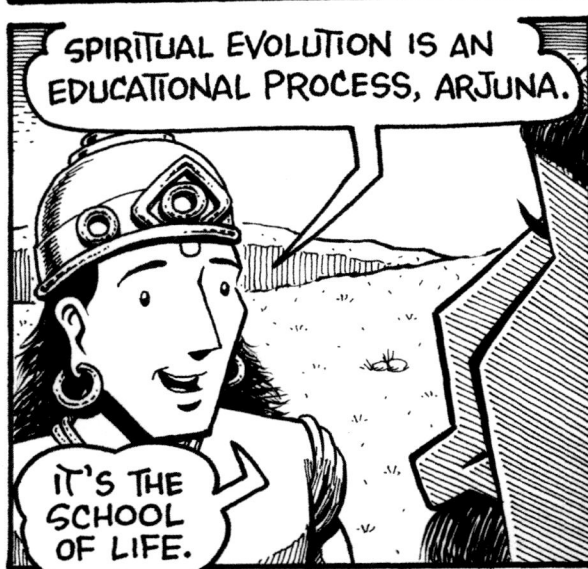

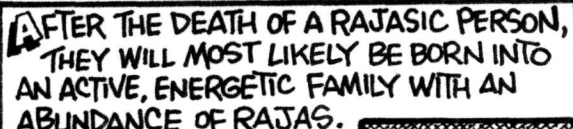

THE NATURE OF THE TAMASIC CHILD IS TO PURSUE MOMENTARY PLEASURE WITH THE LEAST AMOUNT OF EFFORT OR INTERACTION WITH OTHERS.  THE TAMASIC INDIVIDUAL IS NOT INCLINED TO LEARN **ANY** LESSONS FROM LIFE.	THE TAMASIC PERSON IS LIKE SOMEONE WHO SPENDS THEIR ENTIRE LIFE IN A DARKENED ROOM. MANY LIFETIMES COULD HAVE BEEN LIVED IN THIS ROOM, IN THE DARKNESS OF UNAWARENESS.
EVENTUALLY, A BULB WILL SWITCH ON AND, FOR THE FIRST TIME, THIS PERSON WILL BE ABLE TO SEE THE WALLS THAT THEY'VE BEEN BUMPING INTO OVER AND OVER AGAIN FOR AS LONG AS THEY CAN REMEMBER. 	NOW THEY WILL THINK A NEW THOUGHT ABOUT WHAT THEY CAN **DO** TO **STOP** RUNNING INTO THOSE WALLS.  AND THIS IS WHEN TAMAS EVOLVES INTO RAJAS.
INERTIA EVOLVES INTO ACTION. 	THERE WILL COME A TIME WHEN THIS PERSON WILL THINK ***ANOTHER*** NEW THOUGHT. 

CHAPTER 15 - the HIGHER SELF

AND NOW IT'S TIME TO TALK ABOUT THE *TREE* OF *LIFE*.

THIS TREE IS THE SYMBOL OF THE MATERIAL UNIVERSE.

IT REPRESENTS EVERYTHING THAT IS SUBJECT TO CHANGE

THE LEAFY CANOPY OF THE TREE IS ALL THAT WE SEE OR THINK.

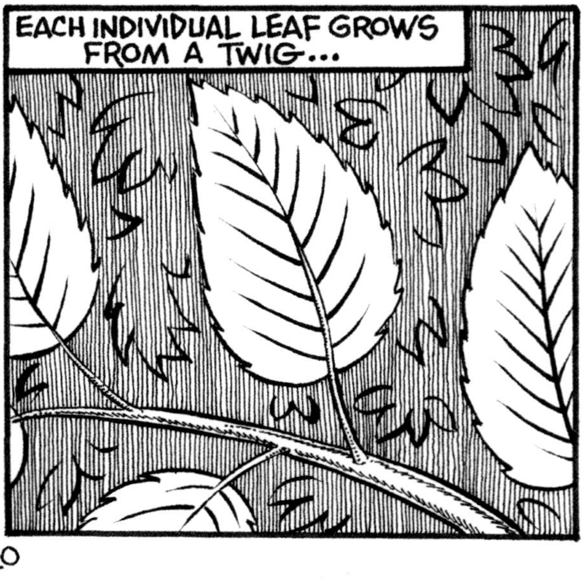

EACH INDIVIDUAL LEAF GROWS FROM A TWIG...

...AND EACH TWIG GROWS FROM A BRANCH...

...EACH BRANCH GROWS FROM THE TREE'S TRUNK...

...AND THE TRUNK GROWS FROM THE TAPROOT, WHICH IS GROUNDED IN THE HIGHER SELF.

WHILE THE TAPROOT OF THE HIGHER SELF NEVER CHANGES, THE TREE'S LEAFY REALM IS IN A STATE OF *CONSTANT* CHANGE.

EACH LEAF FEELS SEPARATE FROM EVERY OTHER LEAF, AND HAS NO AWARENESS OF THE REST OF THE TREE.

IN ASIA, MONKEYS AND BIRDS WILL OFTEN LEAVE THE SEEDS FROM ONE KIND OF TREE UP IN THE BRANCHES OF A *DIFFERENT* TREE.

CHOMP CHOMP CHOMP

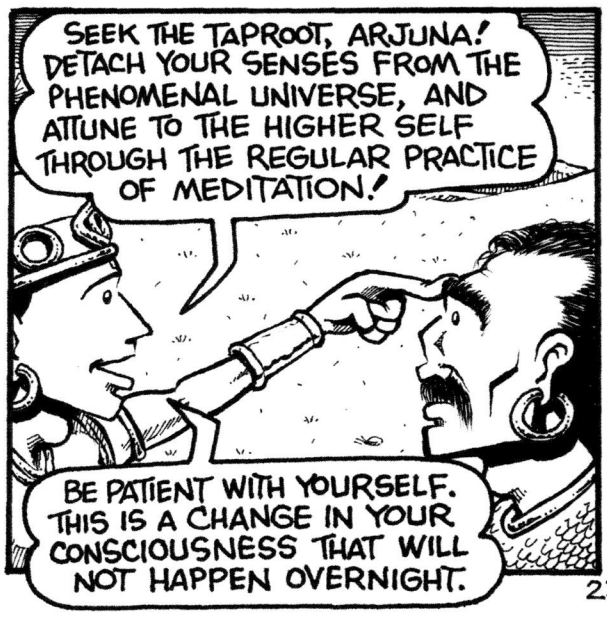

IT IS A GOOD PRACTICE TO HAVE AN IMAGE OF ONE'S DIVINE IDEAL NEARBY AS A REMINDER TO TRY TO THINK, SPEAK, AND ACT AS KRISHNA, JESUS, BUDDHA (OR WHOEVER THE DIVINE IDEAL MIGHT BE) WOULD ACT.

WHEN ONE HAS COMPLETELY IDENTIFIED WITH THEIR DIVINE IDEAL, SAMADHI WILL HAVE BEEN ATTAINED.

WHEN PEOPLE REACH THIS STAGE OF SPIRITUAL EVOLUTION, THEY BECOME COMPASSIONATELY AWARE OF THE FEELINGS OF OTHERS.

THOSE WHO SUCCEED IN THEIR QUEST FOR SELF REALIZATION HAVE A CLEAR UNDERSTANDING OF LIFE.

ATTUNEMENT TO THE HIGHER SELF WILL PROVIDE THEM WITH THE WISDOM NEEDED TO RELIEVE ANY SUFFERING THAT THEY MIGHT ENCOUNTER.

THANK YOU FOR TALKING WITH ME. I FEEL SO MUCH *BETTER* NOW.

THEY HAVE DONE THAT WHICH NEEDED TO BE DONE.

FOR THOSE WHO HAVE FOUND THE TAPROOT TO ETERNAL REALITY, LIFE'S GREATEST GIFT IS THE OPPORTUNITY TO SERVE.

CHAPTER 16 - TWO PATHS

CHAPTER 17 - FAITH

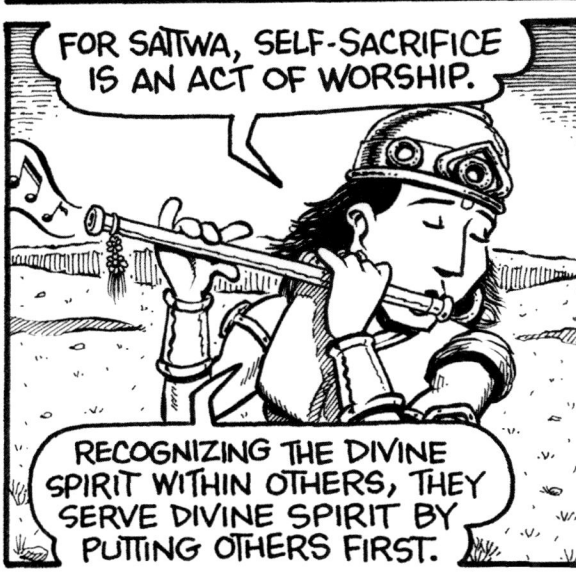

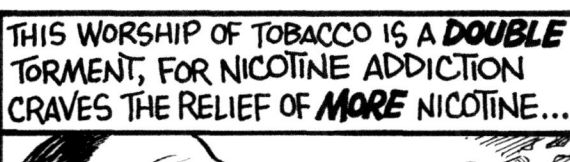

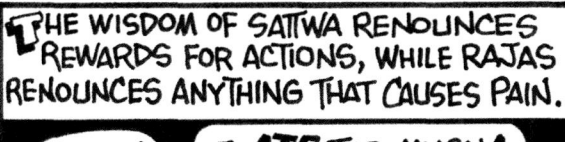

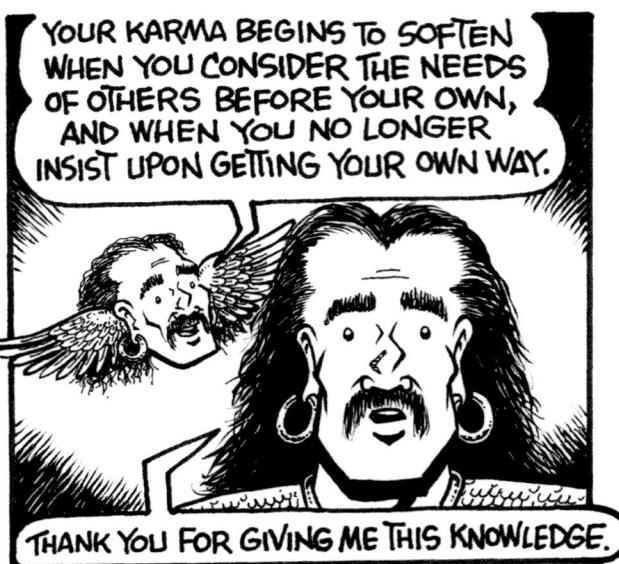

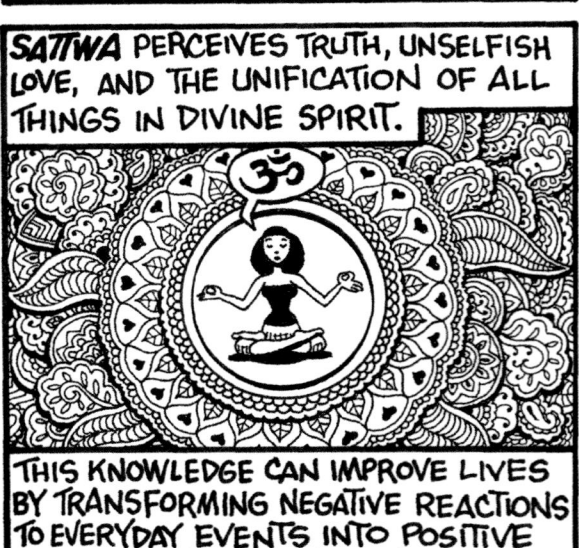

♪ ...UNTIL THE EAGLE GRINS... ♪

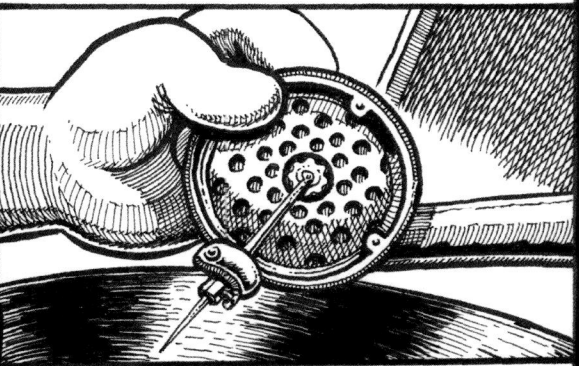
THIS SONG BRINGS US TO THE CONCEPT OF THE WILL.

THE WILL IS WHAT SUSTAINS US IN THOSE TIMES WHEN WE'RE DOWN AND OUT.

WITH A STRONG WILL, WE WON'T FEEL LOST OR ABANDONED DURING LIFE'S MOST CHALLENGING EVENTS.

THANK YOU.

IN A STRONG WILL, WE FIND SUPPORT, CONTENTMENT, AND VITALITY.

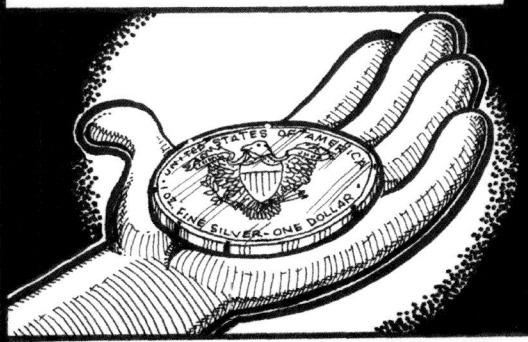
AND IN THE SONG IT'S THE STRONG WILL THAT LOOKS FORWARD TO THE DAY WHEN IT GETS ITS HANDS ON A DOLLAR AGAIN.

THE WILL OF TAMAS IS WEAK AND STUBBORN AFTER SURRENDERING TO FEAR AND LAZINESS.

THIS IS THE SCARIEST MOVIE I'VE EVER *SEEN*, BUT I CAN'T TURN IT *OFF!*

THE WILL OF RAJAS IS DIRECTED TOWARD THE ACQUISITION OF WEALTH, FAME, OR PLEASURE.

NEED A LIFT?

For Rajas, happiness is temporary — part of a cycle in which it alternates with desire.

NOON · 1 PM · 1:30 PM · 2 PM · 3 PM · 3:30 PM · 4 PM · 5 PM · 5:30 PM · 6:00 PM

Happiness for Sattwa comes with the realization that desires are endless, and that their satisfaction is brief.

Sattwic happiness is based on contentment with one's life.

This peace of mind brings an end to sorrow, even in the face of life's most difficult situations.

Self realization is also an acceptance of the immortality of the mind-body complex.

Content with its mortality, yet aware of the conscious immortality at the core of its being, Sattwa chooses to help others find contentment in their lives.

SATTWA REMEMBERS THE MORTALITY THAT TAMAS AND RAJAS HAVE FORGOTTEN.

ARGUING, FIGHTING, OR SELFISH PURSUITS ARE NOT POSSIBILITIES FOR SATTWA, WHO WOULD RATHER BE SERVING OTHERS.

IN AN EARLIER SCENE FROM *THE MAHABHARATA*, YUDHISTHIRA FINDS HIS FOUR BROTHERS (INCLUDING ARJUNA) LYING DEAD BESIDE A SMALL POND.

THE FIVE PANDAVA BROTHERS HAD BEEN LIVING IN EXILE FOR MANY YEARS. AFTER RUNNING OUT OF DRINKING WATER, YUDHISTHIRA SENT HIS BROTHERS OUT, ONE AT A TIME, TO SEARCH FOR A NEW SOURCE OF WATER.

WHEN NONE OF THE BROTHERS RETURNED, YUDHISTHIRA SET OUT TO FIND THEM.

A CRANE IN THE POND BEGINS TO SPEAK...

ALL FOUR OF YOUR BROTHERS REFUSED TO ANSWER MY QUESTIONS BEFORE DRINKING THIS WATER.

BECAUSE OF THIS REFUSAL, THEY HAVE DIED.

AND IF YOU, YUDHISTHIRA, CHOOSE TO ANSWER MY QUESTIONS, YOU MAY DRINK AS MUCH WATER AS YOU WOULD LIKE.

REFUSE AND, LIKE YOUR BROTHERS, YOU SHALL DIE.

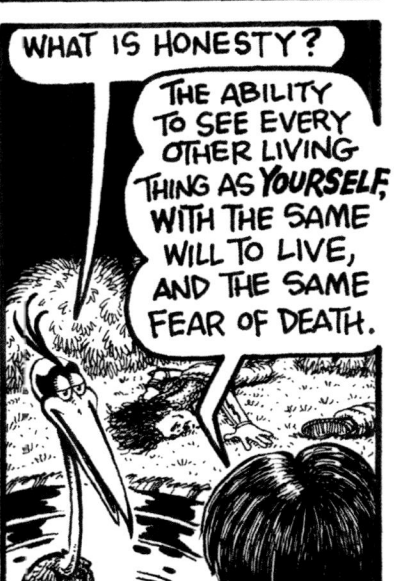

...WHERE TWO OPPOSING ARMIES ARE NOW WAITING FOR KRISHNA AND ARJUNA TO CONCLUDE THEIR DISCUSSION.

IN THE ANCIENT DAYS, FOUR DISTINCT GROUPS WERE FORMED AS THE BASIS OF INDIA'S SOCIAL ORDER.

THESE FOUR GROUPS WERE DESIGNED TO REPRESENT ALL THE DIFFERENT GOALS THAT PEOPLE HAVE IN LIFE, BASED UPON THEIR DOMINANT GUNAS.

THE GROUP AT THE TOP OF THE SOCIAL ORDER WAS COMPOSED OF THOSE DESTINED TO BE PRIESTS, TEACHERS, AND DOCTORS.

THE NATURE OF THIS GROUP WAS TO HAVE SELF-DISCIPLINE, PATIENCE, HUMILITY, AND WISDOM.

THE SECOND GROUP WAS MADE UP OF THOSE WHO WERE STRONG AND COURAGEOUS. LEADERS AND KINGS WERE PART OF THIS GROUP...

...AS WELL AS THE WARRIORS, TRAINED TO NEVER BACK AWAY FROM A BATTLE.

THE THIRD TIER OF THE SOCIAL ORDER CONSISTED OF MERCHANTS, FARMERS, AND ARTISANS.

IT WAS THROUGH THEIR COLLECTIVE VISION, SKILL, AND CREATIVITY THAT ALL THE GROUPS WERE HOUSED, CLOTHED, AND FED.

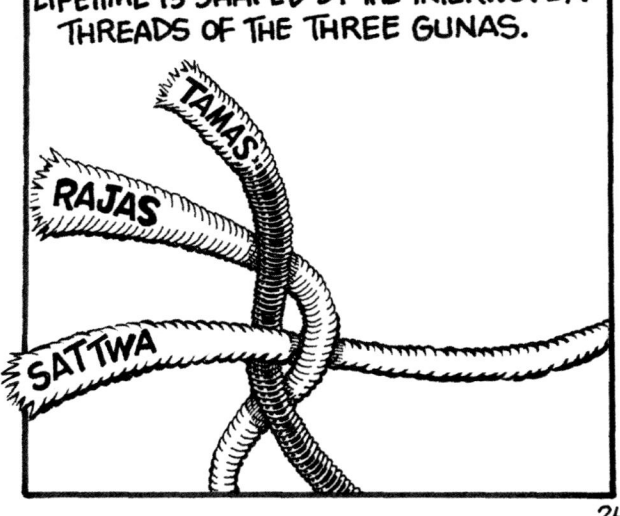
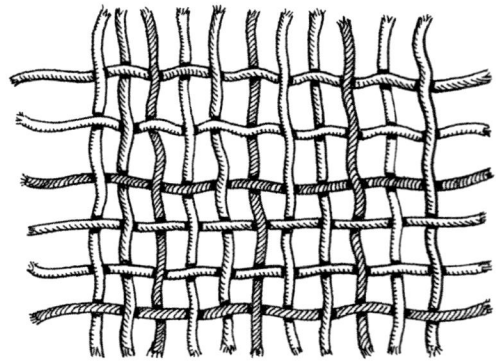

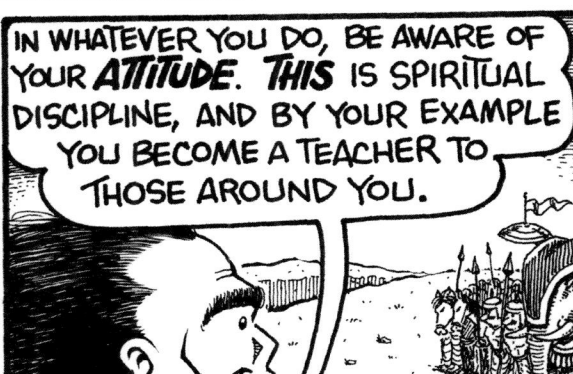

EVERYONE IN THE UNIVERSE OF MIND AND MATTER IS LIVING ON THE WHEEL OF LIFE.

THIS WHEEL IS LIKE A CAROUSEL.

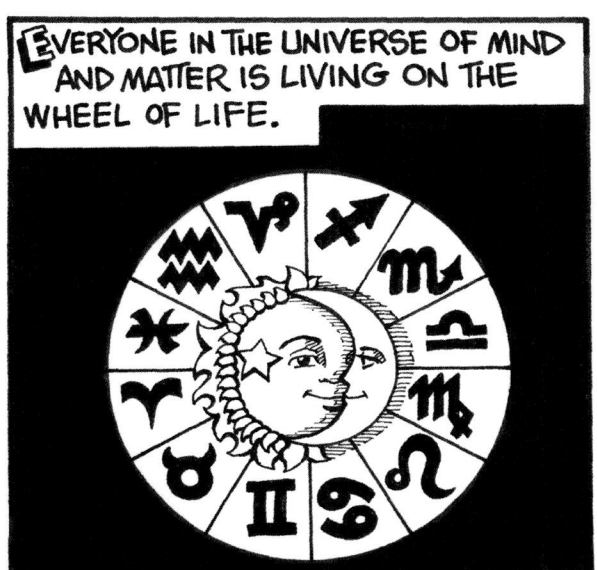

AT BIRTH, EACH PERSON CHOOSES THEIR MOUNT — LION, EAGLE, RAM, BULL — THERE ARE MANY TYPES OF MOUNTS TO CHOOSE FROM.

THE MOUNT ITSELF IS **PRAKRITI** — THE MIND-BODY COMPLEX THAT IS MADE UP OF THE INTERWOVEN THREADS OF THE GUNAS.

EACH PERSON'S CHOICE IS BASED UPON THEIR KARMA.

THE MOUNTS MOVE UP AND DOWN AS THE CAROUSEL SPINS AROUND AND AROUND, CARRYING EACH RIDER FROM BIRTH TO DEATH.

THE CAROUSEL IS MANAGED AND OPERATED BY TIME...

...AND TIME IS A THIEF, SLOWLY ROBBING US OF OUR YOUTH, OUR HEALTH, AND THE PEOPLE AND THINGS THAT WE LOVE.

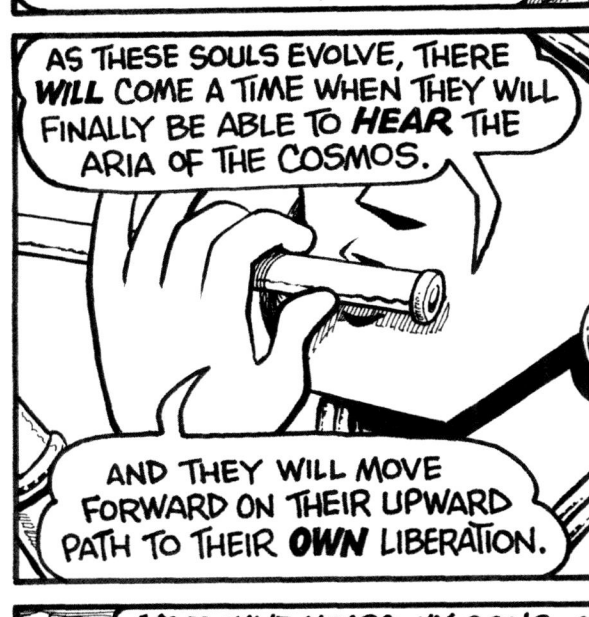

CODA — WRAPPING THINGS UP *MAHABHARATA*-WISE

Just for the record, Arjuna **DID** fight in the Battle of Kurukshetra.

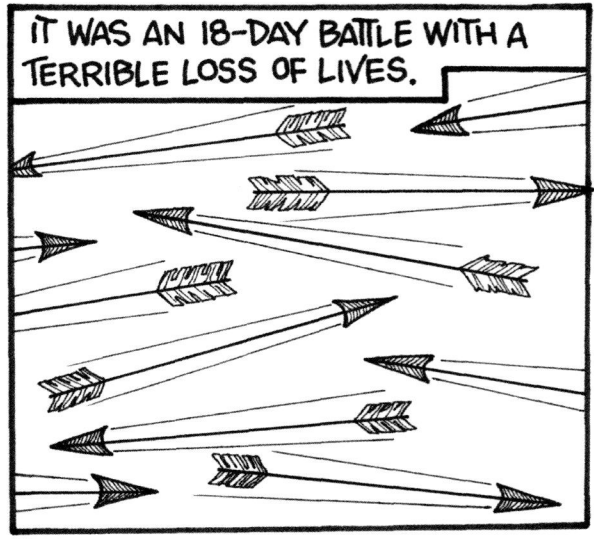

It was an 18-day battle with a terrible loss of lives.

But Arjuna and his four brothers did survive, and the oldest brother, Yudhisthira, did reclaim his throne.

He ruled as a wise and beneficent king for 36 years.

At the end of their lives' journeys, the five Pandava brothers made a pilgrimage to the Himalayas.

They sought to enter Heaven, home of the gods.

Four of the brothers, including Arjuna, died along the way.

Yudhisthira and his faithful dog continued on.

When they reached the gates of Heaven, they were met by Indra, king of the gods.

"**YOU** may enter, Yudhisthira..."

"...but your **DOG** may **NOT**!"

"?!"

EPILOGUE: FINAL WORDS

THE ARJUNA AND KRISHNA OF THE **BHAGAVAD GITA** ARE **DIFFERENT** FROM THEIR COUNTERPARTS IN THE **MAHABHARATA**.

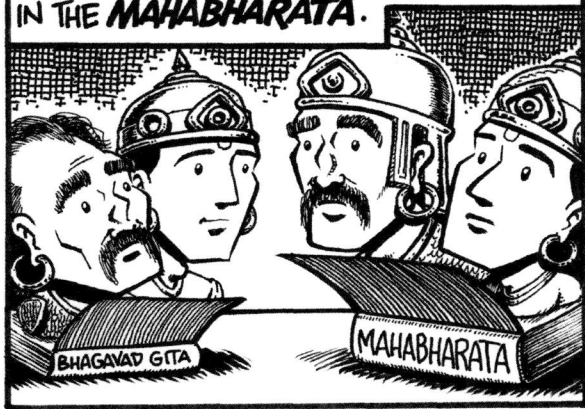

IN THE **GITA**, ARJUNA SYMBOLIZES ANYONE WHO HAS EVER FOUND THEMSELF FIGHTING FOR SURVIVAL ON THE BATTLEFIELD OF MIND AND MATTER.

IN BOTH BOOKS, KRISHNA IS A CHARIOTEER.

THE JOB OF A CHARIOTEER IS TO FIND THE BEST PATHS THROUGH A BATTLE SO THAT THE CHARIOT'S WARRIOR CAN ACT EFFECTIVELY.

IN THE **GITA**, KRISHNA (DIVINE SPIRIT) IS TRYING TO SHOW ARJUNA THE BEST PATHS TO THE SELF-REALIZATION OF SAMADHI, OR, ENLIGHTENMENT.

HIS WORDS GUIDE ARJUNA THROUGH THE FORCES OF LIGHT AND DARKNESS THAT DWELL WITHIN EVERY HUMAN HEART.

IN THE FINITE LIFE OF THE HUMAN, THERE IS A NATURAL LONGING FOR THE INFINITE.

ALL THE BEAUTY THAT'S EVER BEEN CAPTURED IN MUSIC, ART, AND POETRY IS AN EXPRESSION OF THIS LONGING.

SPIRITUAL EVOLUTION IS THE RESULT OF A TRANSCENDENT GRAVITY PULLING THE INDIVIDUAL SOUL TOWARD A FINAL REUNION WITH DIVINE SPIRIT.